KILL THE TSAR!

YOUTH AND TERRORISM IN OLD RUSSIA

KILL THE TSAR!

YOUTH AND TERRORISM IN OLD RUSSIA

K. C. TESSENDORF

ATHENEUM   1986   NEW YORK

The illustrations on pages, 24, 44, 48,
50-51, 63, 73, 78-79, 106-07, 108-09, 112, 115, and 117
courtesy of The Library of Congress.

Library of Congress Cataloging-in-Publication Data
Tessendorf, K. C.   Kill the tsar.
Bibliography: p. 123.
Includes index.
SUMMARY: Examines the comparatively liberal reign of Alexander II
of Russia and the concurrent actions of radicals and terrorists,
who sought political reforms and eventually assassinated him.
1. Soviet Union—Politics and government—1855-1881—Juvenile
literature. 2. Alexander II, Emperor of Russia, 1818-1881—
Assassination—Juvenile literature.
3. Terrorism—Soviet Union—History—19th century—Juvenile literature.
[1. Soviet Union—Politics and government—1855-1881.
2. Alexander II, Emperor of Russia, 1818-1881. 3. Terrorism—
Soviet Union—History—19th century] I. Title.
DK221.T47   1986   947.08'1   85-27494
ISBN 0-689-31124-9

Copyright © 1986 by K. C. Tessendorf
All rights reserved
Published simultaneously in Canada by
Collier Macmillan Canada, Inc.
Type set by Maryland Linotype, Baltimore, Maryland
Printed and bound by Fairfield Graphic, Fairfield, Pennsylvania
Designed by Marjorie Zaum
First Edition

To my scholarly predecessors for developing a wealth of material on the persons, plots, and incidents culminating in the assassination of Alexander II, and to the Library of Congress for gathering and preserving it.

CONTENTS

INTRODUCTION: Tsaricide 3

    I: The Children of Chernyshevsky 7
    II: Lambs Into Wolves 26
    III: The Turn Toward Terrorism 46
    IV: The Siege Of The Winter Palace 69
    V: Execution! 95

CONCLUSION: Afterward 119
A Popular Bibliography 123
Index 125

Don't let anyone tell us that we—but a small band—are too weak to attain unto the magnificent end at which we aim. Count and see how many there are who suffer this injustice. We peasants who work for others, and who mumble the straw while our master eats the wheat, we by ourselves are millions of men. We workers who weave silks and velvet in order that we may be clothed in rags, we, too, are a great multitude; and when the clang of the factories permits us a moment's repose, we overflow the streets and squares like the sea in a spring tide. We soldiers who are driven along to the word of command, or by blows, we who receive the bullets for which our officers get crosses and pensions, we, too, poor fools who have hitherto known no better than to shoot our brothers, why we have only to make a right about-face towards those plumed and decorated personages who are so good as to command us, to see a ghastly pallor overspread their faces.

Ay, all of us together, we who suffer and are insulted daily, we are a multitude whom no man can number, we are the ocean that can embrace and swallow up all else. When we have but the will to do it, that very moment will justice be done: that very instant the tyrants of the earth shall bite the dust.

—Prince Peter Kropotkin
Russian Revolutionary
Publicist

KILL THE TSAR!

YOUTH AND TERRORISM IN OLD RUSSIA

Introduction
Tsaricide

The vehicles, common wooden carts upon which temporary benches had been secured, creaked through the early morning streets of St. Petersburg, their human cargo swaying in jerky unison as the springless wagons jolted over the cobblestones and splashed through slushy puddles. Long, monotonous drumrolls arose from an accompanying army unit. The drummers were present to overwhelm with sound any attempt by the captives to address the mildly hostile crowd lining the route to the execution ground.

The prisoners were lashed to their seats facing backward; two men in the first cart, a trio behind in the other. The central figure here, a petite young woman of deceptively childlike appearance, attracted notice. About the shoulders of each captive was draped a placard on which was starkly written in dripping letters:

TSARICIDE

It was the 3rd of April, 1881, and these five young people were shortly to be hanged for plotting and committing the assassination of Tsar Alexander II, known to history as Old Russia's "Tsar Liberator."

Repeatedly the young woman twisted to look fervently toward the more striking of the two men in the first cart. He sat proudly erect and disdainful of his cowering companion. His was a strong, magnetic face framed by a wild cascading beard and long hair flowing in the wind. The glances the man and woman exchanged were confident renewals of their love as well as stoic courage to the end.

They were Andrei Zhelyabov, thirty, and Sophia (Sonia) Perovskaya, twenty-six, leaders and veteran members of the terrorist group that committed the regicide. Both had spent their teen and adult years in dissent, revolutionary activism and finally terrorism. Their revolutionary band, "The People's Will," had in fact sentenced Alexander II to death at a session two years before and Zhelyabov and Perovskaya had participated in the planning and action of most of the failed attempts to kill

April 3, 1881, St. Petersburg: Five members of "The People's Will" journey to their execution for the assassination of Tsar Alexander II. (Sketch published in The London Illustrated News, *supplement, April 30, 1881.*)

KILL THE TSAR

the tsar that preceded his assassination on March 1, 1881.

Terrorism is the terrible tool used by small factions that can't gain political prominence through ordinary means. They plot and perform political executions and are willing to kill innocent persons to attain their goals. They are the ultimate fanatical endorsers of the credo: *The end justifies the means.*

The People's Will believed murder was moral if it moved "the people" toward political power, and were naive enough to think that a great popular revolt would sweep Russia when it was known the tsar had been executed by their hands.

Nothing of the sort happened. Outrage and suspicion of treason were the reaction of "the people" and the new tsar was far more repressive than his father. Popular politics in Russia were put in deep freeze for the next quarter century. The will of The People's Will appeared to have utterly failed.

Yet the killing of the tsar is a noteworthy marker pointing toward our own times. It is possible that St. Petersburg of Old Russia became the Leningrad of the USSR because of what was done by the terrorist assassins on that winter day a century ago.

Alexander II was the most liberal tsar who had ruled Old Russia. He proposed and enacted personal freedom for many millions of Russian serfs (slaves). And despite the constant death threat of the terrorists, he had signed a decree on the eve of his death day that allowed a small beginning toward constitutional rule. The terrorist bombs killed the ruler who would have been most likely to oversee an orderly easing of Russian official repression.

Why did they kill him? Who were these terrorists who presumed to call themselves "The People's Will?" How did Andrei and Sonia come to follow the bloody revolutionary road to the St. Petersburg scaffold?

I
THE CHILDREN OF CHERNYSHEVSKY

Andrei and Sonia were children of the Russian sixties. They grew to their age of political awareness in the most exciting, disturbing decade that Old Russia had experienced in centuries. It was a time when—for a few years—it really seemed that anything might be possible in a new Russia, painfully changing to keep up with Western Europe and America. This modernization of the government, ambitiously begun by Tsar Alexander II with the liberation of more than twenty-five million serfs, provided for ambitious young people such as Andrei and Sonia a choice in life-styles unthought of a few years earlier.

In the Emancipation year of 1861 Andrei Zhelyabov was a serf child eleven years old. Because of overcrowding at home he had been sent to spend five years living with his grandparents who were land serfs in another part of southern Russia.

The elder grandfather, self-instructed and devoted to religious literature, was attracted to his grandson and taught the lad to read the old church script and psalms.

Any level of literacy was rare in the peasantry, but young Andrei remained a serf, and in the 1850s that was a slave. His dull future was in the hands of his master to whom the serf was a number in an account book. Estates of that era were not valued by acreage but by the number of "souls" the landlord owned. Serfdom may be divided into three general divisions: those who worked the vast agricultural lands of Russia, those who were employed in the master's household or estate shops, and those who were put out to work in the cities in industrial or service occupations. This latter arrangement, called *obrok*, may be used to show why serf owners were unwilling to have the system changed.

Supposing you were a landowner and through inheritance or position owned five serfs who, being surplus for work on your land, were sent to a big city to work in a factory. You never saw or communicated with them, probably didn't even know their names. Yet all of their earnings except the very bare minimum necessary to feed and shelter them was sent to you. It would be an arrangement very hard for you to let loose of when "it's always been like that."

Why would the serfs put up with this when they were so many and their masters so few?

The serf masses were illiterate, ignorant, beaten down by centuries of brutality and neglect and thereby completely unorganized. Their everlasting poverty and demoralization blunted their motivation. The occasional instances of rebellion were put down by public floggings, by exile to Siberia, or by the owner

The Children of Chernyshevsky

turning the troublemakers over to the army, a cruel life sentence—twenty-five years at least.

Over many generations the serfs had kept sanity by steadfastly maintaining a faith in God and in the goodness of their distant "little father," the tsar. They believed that if *he* only knew what villains and oppressors his landowners were, surely one day he would come and set them free and give them the land they lived on.

That was wishful thinking, while in stark reality the serf had no standing in national law, no personal choice in occupation, place of residence or even whom he or she would marry. The owner was the final authority. As the master desired, the serf was ordered about, moved, separated from family, uplifted or debased, rewarded or punished. It helped of course to have a kindly master, but in any case there was no appeal or relief from his decisions.

Andrei understood before he was ten what it was like to endure a hard master. While he was living with his grandfather, the owner raped the boy's favorite aunt. His grandfather reported the offense to the local police, a very brave thing to do in those days. Nothing came of it—probably the owner was considered master of his property in a legal sense. Morality was a matter of private choice for the master. With childish fury Andrei resolved to return when grown and kill the man.

About the time that Andrei returned to his parents, the Emancipation of the serfs took effect. It was a compromise between the tsar and the serf owners (the serfs were of course not consulted) in the matter of land distribution. The serfs would have to pay (over thirty years) the government for their land. Meanwhile the government recompensed the grumbling landowners with long-term bonds. But the social and legal concept of serf/slave had been abolished; they had standing and rights—not yet great, but real—before the national law. A great watershed of human rights was crossed without a revolution. By patched-up compromise a great civil war, like the one just beginning in the United States, had been avoided.

Back at home with his parents, who were house serfs, now servants (which placed them in close contact with their landlord), Andrei's brightness and bit of book learning were noticed by the former owner, now employer, a progressive man who took enough interest, in this new era, to send the peasant boy to school. Andrei did well enough there to secure a scholarship and went on to a university to study law.

A serf sent to law school? That surely was an unlikely dream in former times. Without Alexander's reforms, Andrei would have spent his life as a serf. Since he showed an unruly and trouble-seeking disposition from his teens onward, he might have been one of the serfs committed to a life sentence in the army.

By contrast, Sonia Perovskaya, seven in 1861, was a daughter of the highest aristocracy. The family tree was particularly exalted on her mother's side. Her father, a politically ambitious general, was poorer and lower in family pedigree. His inherently surly and tyrannical disposition was made more so by feelings of inferiority. The couple were the battling Perovskis at home. The wife, strong-willed also, stood up to her husband as best she could. Sonia, inheriting obstinate independence from both parents, early on sided with her mother and grew up despising her father, an attitude she applied more mildly to all other men for many years.

Somewhat aided by her mother, Sonia in her teens strove to become one of the "new people" of her generation. She was

The Children of Chernyshevsky

able to enroll in a progressive school where she received training as a physician's assistant and teacher, and participated actively in student intellectual circles.

Access of Russian women to meaningful education was primarily another reform of Alexander II. For generations a daughter of the nobility normally received only a domestic finishing school education—how to become an exemplary wife, mother and homemaker. The Russian writer Gogol has satirized upper class boarding school curriculum as:

> . . . the French language, indispensible to family happiness; the pianoforte, to afford pleasant moments to one's spouse; . . . knitting of purses and other presents with which to surprise one's husband.

From such a fate Sonia and many other determined young Russian women found opportunity to escape in the heady decade of the sixties.

Though both Andrei and Sonia chose to turn to professional political agitation, they would otherwise have emerged as trained professionals in law and health education, occupations not available to their stations in society in Old Russia.

Alexander II's educational reforms had the objective of training professionals to run modern Russia, and the majority (too dull and predictable to be much recorded in history) of Russian university students fulfilled this intent. But the atmosphere of free thought necessary in an intelligent educational process also turned out political malcontents. The numbers of radicalized youth, though always relatively few, were increasing, to the dismay of nearly everyone but themselves.

Alexander II had loosened censorship and greatly broadened and freed the educational process. In immediate response charismatic spokesmen appeared to speak out to a young audience eager to listen. And the message given out was: Freedom . . . Justice . . . More! More!

In a celebrated novel, *Fathers and Sons*, Ivan Turgenev tagged the professionals of this dawning counterculture as "nihilists." They were political activists who rejected "reform" and felt the entire social/governmental structure must be blown away and something new and radical erected in its place.

The feelings of these young Russian nihilists about human rights and equality was intense and impatient. They saw the present system as a terrible offender against human rights and wanted to abolish it. Dmitry Pisarov, a nihilist propagandist, urged:

> *This is the final word of our young camp: What can be broken, we should break. Whatever will stand the blow—is of use; whatever will be smashed to pieces—is rubbish. At any rate smash right and left, no harm may come of this.*

The political radicalism of the young caused colossal generation gaps to open in their family life. In an adult society as stuffed with conservative tradition as Old Russia's, the extremity of the doctrine of youth dissent made it absolutely unacceptable, unimaginable even, to the elders. In many families a harsh parting of paths and households occurred.

Here in this Russian setting of just one hundred-plus years ago were developed the counterculture attitudes and styles that, flourishing then for a few years, would be renewed in the time

The Children of Chernyshevsky

of the Communist Revolution, and once again become the role models of the radicals of the 1960s.

Certainly young Russia publicly flaunted its independent tastes. Their dress displayed their separation from conventional society and their kinship to each other. The men sported well-worn laborer's clothing—with a red shirt and blue-tinted glasses perhaps—and long hair and smooth-shaven cheeks (beards were then officially in favor). No mistaking them for some wimp of a government bureaucrat!

The women with hair cut short wore plain dresses, men's boots, tinted glasses and perhaps flourished a cigarette! An annoyed police observer wrote that they probably lived "in the company of a similarly repulsive individual of the male sex, or with several of them."

The tsar was piqued and unable to comprehend why in his era of reform this class should appear. He did not understand how a little freedom let loose in a clamped-down, authoritarian society could release a yearning for more, or for complete freedom, among idealistic young people who still believe anything is possible in their lifetimes. This was in part because Tsar Alexander II was not really interested in "freedom" at all.

A pliable man, Alexander had listened to a liberal tutor in youth, had married a liberal German princess, and at the beginning of his reign had followed the advice of a liberal brother and the rare members of the nobility who were like-minded. He had entered with great enthusiasm into his era of reform. But his sole reason for reform was to help the imperial Russian state cope with a modern world it had neither made nor understood.

Alexander remained a true autocrat. He agreed with the peasantry—he saw nothing wrong with the "God and the Tsar" principle so long as the tsar ruled with gracious, far-seeing wisdom as he trusted he was doing. And he alone was the proper instigator of any reform. Very respectfully offered counsel would be considered, but he alone would decide.

While the tsar remained bewildered all his life at the actions of the radicals in the same way that their parents did, those in authority in the middle and lower levels of his government detested the nihilists and regarded them as natural enemies. The tendency would always be strong, often overwhelming, to restrain, harass, or jail these young rebels whose very appearance was a planned insult to traditional society.

The revived Russian universities were the headquarters, the message centers and flash points of radicalism. The on again/off again academic freedom allowed by the government, and the organizational activities of the students made for a hectic time for college administrators in the 1860s—calming suspicious authorities on the one hand and dealing with strident student demands on the other.

The radical students aimed "to shake up with their original skepticism those stale objects, that dilapidated junk" of the traditional curriculum. The academic atmosphere was turbulent with a "spirit of criticism, self-will and youthful pugnaciousness toward the professors. . . . It became customary in the classes to applaud, to whistle, to hiss."

Overindulgence produced overreaction. In October of 1861, the Minister of Education put into force at the St. Petersburg University a series of rules hampering student organization or assembly. Mass meetings and marches resulted. The school was closed and student leaders arrested. This action prompted more meetings, which were dispersed by troops. Then the authorities

Tsar Alexander II. (Sketch published in the French magazine, L'Illustration, Journal Universel, *March 19, 1881.)*

began arresting students and soon had three hundred of them jailed.

Alexander II was in the far south at the time and immediately set out for St. Petersburg. As the royal coach-and-four galloped northward (railways, an economic reform of the tsar, were beginning to be built but had not yet reached the south), someone took a shot at the travelers, the first of several bullets to whistle near the emperor. Arriving in the capital, he ordered the students released, and relieved both the education chief and the governor general of the province, replacing them with liberal administrators.

Then, in the summer of 1862, the large cities of Russia began to burn. The police could not identify the arsonists but there was a general suspicion. The writer Turgenev arrived in St. Petersburg on the day of its worst fire, ". . . and the word 'nihilist' was on everybody's lips. A friend I met on the Nevsky said to me— 'Look what *your* nihilists are doing! There is arson all over St. Petersburg.' "

Indeed there was. The fires continued for a week, burning at least a quarter of the capital. The accused radical faction retorted that these were police fires set to discredit them. Perhaps so—it is still a mystery—but the Russian public, tiring of unruly youth and its radical talk, chose to believe the destruction was an illustration of nihilist doctrine.

In the aftermath of ashes and the public's conservative turn of mood the police took opportunity to jail on general principles several of the natural leaders. The most notable of these was the popular liberal intellectual N. G. Chernyshevsky. They locked him up for eight months before charging him with writing a handbill that blamed the tsar himself for obstruction in land

The Children of Chernyshevsky

distribution to the ex-serfs. The handbill was unsigned. Modern scholarship is inclined toward his authorship.

This "saintly revolutionary" was a priest's son of great intellect and ambition. When very young he had thought to master all human knowledge and write an encyclopedia. Later he spent a couple of years trying to master the puzzling principle of perpetual motion. Now, slightly over thirty, he was a university and literary personage of importance, one of the (careful) liberal voices raised within pre-Emancipation Russia who had succeeded in being an adviser to the liberal faction and escaping imprisonment until the fall of 1862.

The jailed genius, separated from his family, believed he would go stir crazy unless he could at least continue his literary activities. The prison warden allowed him to convert his cell into a library stacked to its ceiling with books and papers. He wrote at a rapid pace—articles, essays, and translations of important foreign books. All passed the censors into publication. Then he began a novel and in feverish inspiration finished it in four months.

What Is to Be Done? didn't have a smooth literary style because its plot was formed to suit the writer's moral purposes. Yet this novel was a blockbuster. It would deeply impress and motivate the "new people" in Russia for generations to come (the youthful Lenin read it six times in one summer).

What Is To Be Done? did not mention the government or any authority, but attacked all the foundations of Old Russia. It depicted a race of new people, the dedicated idealistic young men and women of the nation, who, soon arising and multiplying over coming decades, would overcome all selfish evil with rational good.

In the book this new force is personified by a selfless nihilist who is a superhero idolized by his peers. He is so intent on self-conditioning that one night he sleeps bloodily on a bed of nails to improve his confidence in his toughness.

The plot, an extended parable, concerns a student doctor who rescues by fake marriage the teen-age heroine from a hopelessly traditional family situation. They live in a three room flat—his, hers, and a neutral room used for elevating conversations. Their rooms are distinctly private. The characters are not prudes; rather sex is unthought of amid the earnest talk about social uplift for the masses.

So inspired, the heroine is successful in planning and organizing a labor cooperative in the dressmaking trade. Meanwhile, she decides she would prefer future meditation with another man, also a young physician. So the husband doctor obligingly fakes suicide so that the "widow" may legally remarry. She does so and is soon in school studying medicine herself. At the same time doctor number one, the "suicide," encounters and marries the woman that doctor number two left behind when he married the "widow" of doctor number one. At book's end Chernyshevsky's romantic quadrangle is living helpfully together and daily going out to work among the masses.

Through a bureaucratic foul-up of censors with overlapping duties, *What Is To Be Done?* was not officially reviewed, but was passed and published and became an immediate sensation. The book was then banned, which of course increased its notoriety.

The story responded to the need of young, altruistic Russia expressed in the plea: "We are seeking, thirsting, waiting. We are waiting for someone to tell us what to do."

The Children of Chernyshevsky

Chernyshevsky's call to participation in social revolution was personal and ringing: "You are the best among the best, the movers of movers, the salt of the salt of the earth!" The public-spirited youth of Russia hastened to accept and believe in this exhilarating challenge.

Twenty months after his imprisonment Chernyshevsky was tried and sentenced to seven years of Siberian imprisonment. The charge of seditious writing was not proven, but the government would not free a man whom they had come to regard as among the most dangerous to Old Russia.

Just before the Siberian journey the prisoner was subjected to a "civic execution." On a platform before a crowd the convict was symbolically cast out of society as a sword was broken over his head (mock execution) and he was chained to a post (restraint from society, imprisonment).

It was raining that day and as the soaked Chernyshevsky stood in chains on the platform looking out in forlorn dignity to the umbrella-shielded people a remarkable gesture occurred. At this point the crowd was expected to boo the prisoner. But there was a humane silence, only the sodden beat of the rain continuing. Then a flower bouquet arched from the crowd onto the platform—and another followed! As the flabbergasted police reacted, a third floral tribute arrived. They captured the thrower, a seventeen-year-old girl known to history only as "Michaelis." For her brave gesture she was banished permanently from St. Petersburg.

Chernyshevsky was not allowed to return to European Russia till twenty years had passed, and so was unable to lead the "new people." There were plenty of imaginative radicals in Russia, and outside, to take his model forward. But the various

Convicted of "seditious writing," N.G. Chernyshevsky was sentenced to imprisonment in Siberia. On his way there, he was subjected to a symbolic "civic execution." (Sketch published in Alexander I and II *by Mikhail Gershenvov, 1911.)*

The Children of Chernyshevsky

programs for social revolution differed in goals and methods and leadership. The failure to get together behind a single charismatic leader and a common program made the prospect of political success unreasonable.

Among the splinter of conspiratorial groups formed all over Russia in the mid sixties was a Moscow cell called "The Organization." It was the brainchild of two foster brothers of the minor nobility who were college dropouts in their mid-twenties. Nikolai Ishutin was the theorist and Dimitri Karakozov became its flamboyant activist. The small group lived ascetic lives in commune quarters and followed the gospel of *What Is to Be Done?* literally, working at labor organizing and opening free schools for city workers. A dressmaker's cooperative was among the projects modeled on the book. Yet no women were invited to join The Organization.

On the dark side, the group had a special secret division called "Hell," where political assassination was avidly studied. The members of Hell lived anonymous lives under false names and severed all social contacts with their past. The leader, at the right time, would choose the target and the members of Hell would draw lots. The designated assassin would disfigure his face with acid immediately before the attempt and swallow poison immediately afterward.

Ishutin was vague about when Hell would be unleashed—sometime in the future when the movement had gathered popular support. Meanwhile it was exciting to inflame the imaginations of the would-be terrorists.

Karakozov, teaching in a free school, was a moody young man. He knew about Hell, and when he became sickly and was told he probably would not live long, this nihilist decided to be Hell's assassin, to leave this political statement as his grave marker. Karakozov reasoned that the lack of social justice and its accompanying repression in Russia must be the fault of Alexander II. He would kill the tsar!

Ishutin tried to talk his friend out of it. It was too soon; The Organization was not ready. He might spoil everything for its future! But Karakozov bought a pistol, some poison and took the train to St. Petersburg.

April 16, 1866, was Ossip Kommissarov's Saint's Day, therefore a personal holiday. The ex-serf was employed as a hatter in St. Petersburg. He decided to spend part of his day off mingling with royalty! He joined the small crowd clustered before the emperor's carriage at the gate of the palace gardens. Alexander II was taking a spring ramble there with a few friends. Soon the tsar emerged and passed within a yard of the gaping Kommissarov. It was almost like being in heaven!

Now the monarch paused before the carriage as a valet laid a cape upon the royal shoulders. Someone rudely shoved past the adoring peasant, who looked up in irritation and saw an arm extended with a pistol pointed at the nape of the imperial neck! Quick as a flash he batted at the arm. The pistol cracked but the bullet went wide. The crowd pinned Karakozov against the garden fence and began beating and tearing at him as he exclaimed:

"You fools! I did it for you."

Alexander II was a model of composure. He waited to interview the assassin, a practice which would become fatal in the future.

The police secured the captive, and the emperor, who had two years ago put down a revolt by the Polish nobility, asked coolly: "Are you a Pole?"

The Children of Chernyshevsky

"No, pure Russian!" was the proud reply.

"Why did you fire the pistol?"

"Look at the freedom you have given the peasants . . ." Karakozov appeared choked with bitterness and said no more.

The Emperor thanked the quick-handed hatter and promised reward. Then he walked to a nearby cathedral to personally thank God for his survival. At least ninety-five percent of the Russian people shared in that sentiment.

Sonia Perovskaya was still a child, now eleven, but the Karakozov attempt affected her family life. Her father had capped his political career by becoming governor of St. Petersburg. Now he was among the scapegoats shaken out after the shooting and he lost his position. General Perovski had run up sizable debts on the unlimited credit his office afforded. He could not immediately pay up, and the family temporarily separated, with Sonia going with her mother to that family's Crimean estates.

Also in the south, Andrei Zhelyabov, now fifteen, had grown tall and handsome, with a magnetic personality. He was also unruly, a trouble-seeker drawn to revolutionary agitation at school. He expressed excitement at the bravado of the assassin and was sorry the bold stroke had failed.

Though Karakozov refused for a week to even reveal his name, the police were able, with the aid of his hotel-keeper, to backtrack him to The Organization, Ishutin and coconspirators. There were about twenty in all. Ishutin pleaded that Karakozov had acted on his own, but it did not suit the police to believe him. A conspiracy theory better fitted their objective.

Karakozov was hanged. Ishutin received a hardcore "civic execution" meaning he mounted a scaffold expecting to be

Ossip Ivanovich Kommissarov, a former serf, saved Tsar Alexander II from the assassination attempt of Dimitri Karakozov of The Organization. (Sketch published in L'Illustration, late spring 1866.)

The Children of Chernyshevsky

hanged, was reprieved to prison with the rope around his neck! The Organization was no more. Ossip Kommissarov, savior of the tsar, was made a noble, entertained at the tsar's Winter Palace. A simple fellow, he could not readjust his personality to the new high life style. He became an ill-spoken social bore and was encouraged to retire to the country estate the grateful monarch provided him. There he faded from public notice into the mists of alcoholism.

The conservative majority of nobles near the tsar now stepped boldly forward. They showed him various inflammatory handbills calling for his death and supposed evidence of scores of revolutionary cells. They argued forcefully that the era of reform he had sponsored had spawned this swarm of potential terrorists.

Alexander II listened to them. He was not afraid and said he did not sustain personal anger against the radical revolutionists. But he was convinced by the conservatives and the police that the state, traditional Holy Russia, was endangered. His decision to shut down (but not cancel) the reforms—he placed conservatives in charge—was understandably human, but not that of a far-seeing statesman.

The tsar was sorely disillusioned. It seemed that his labors had resulted only in making the new Russia "an incomplete and uncomfortable dwelling, where friends and opponents of innovation felt almost equally ill at ease."

In the next year, 1867, while Alexander II was on a state visit to France, a Pole fired two pistol shots at him as he rode in an open carriage with Napoleon III. The French emperor cowered but the tsar was resolute. In St. Petersburg a legend began to form that Alexander had divine protection.

II

LAMBS INTO WOLVES

The official repression that followed Karakozov's assassination attempt in 1866 was often mindless and inefficiently mounted. The tsar and his conservative advisers became almost paranoiac in their resistance to change. A citizen who stood up to make a suggestion of how to do anything better in civil affairs risked a ticket to Siberia. The state was incapable, often, of discerning its enemies. Instead it swept up in its police net many persons whose "crime" was an earnest, honest desire to aid or instruct other Russians. Guilt by association was *in*.

The government's behavior demanded a response from the critics of the regime. Continued defiance had become illegal—it was time to retire, or to go underground. The majority of liberals in Russia, those older and established in careers, decided to be cautious. They abhorred revolution with its radical and sudden changes in society as well as government. They hoped that if they were patient and reasonable the tsar might again venture into reform, into the beginnings of representative government. They felt the system should be changed from within by careful adjustments.

Not so with the children of Chernyshevsky! This small but very intense faction remained radical and in a hurry. However their self-image and objectives had subtly shifted. The phase of social revolution, in which they had been preoccupied with escape from parental restraint, and with the planning of their own education and future careers was ending. Now they aspired to be "populists," persons dedicated to raising to political consciousness the millions of peasants and the industrial workers in the cities—the People. Sonia Perovskaya would soon become a leader, a purist of the pure in word and deed, within the populist movement.

In 1869, the southern estate, which had been a refuge to Sonia and her mother, was sold to pay family debts and they returned to St. Petersburg and life with father. It seems the family atmosphere became more combative than before. Tyranny clashed with rebellion. The mother succeeded in placing Sonia in a type of junior women's college (a reform of Alexander II) where a teacher's certificate could be earned. In the style of the heroine of *What Is to Be Done?* Sonia chose health education.

The idea of women's professional education must have seemed absurd and dangerous to Sonia's father. But Sonia prospered at school while her father exhausted himself in his family role of rule or ruin. He became ill and decided on a summer's sojourn at European spas. Perovski's wife and other daughter accompanied him, but not Sonia. She had an invitation to spend the summer at the home of school friends. Perhaps the father believed the best medicine of all would be a few months separation from his stubborn daughter!

Sonia's friends were the three Kornilov sisters, daughters of a wealthy and very liberal merchant family. And it was with them that she began to read "the thick journals" and became familiar with the literature of dissent, and with the worth of personal and political freedom. When the Perovski family returned to St. Petersburg, Sonia refused to go home. Father insisted and threatened police action. So before she was sixteen, Sonia entered the semi-underground of student activism. General Perovski, when he was convinced the tsar's police could not find her, most reluctantly allowed her independence. Sonia's visits to her beloved mother became secret occasions, and she may never have seen her father again.

A photograph of Sonia with her school friends shows a girl young enough in appearance to be an eighth grader. She seems "girlhood personified" but very serious. A young woman who first saw her at a political soirée the Kornilovs were hosting in the early days recalled her as standing out in the group because of her appearance and demeanor. Though the others were attired in the colorful radical chic of the time (red "Garibaldi" sashes modeled on the famous Italian revolutionary, etc.) Sonia "totally oblivious of her appearance" wore a plain gray dress with a white collar, almost a schoolgirl's uniform. Blondish, a broad, high forehead was the most imposing feature of her blue-eyed, rounded face. The diminutive Sonia was engaged in a political argument with a taller girl and was reacting with extreme restraint but righteous intensity.

> *Her expression was distrustful. When she was silent her small, childlike mouth was tightly shut, as if she*

Lambs Into Wolves

feared saying something superfluous. Her face was deeply thoughtful and serious; her entire figure exuded a monastic asceticism . . . this girl resembled one of those stubborn defenders of their faith who carry their cause to the point of self-annihilation . . .

Sharply focused eye-level appraisals of Sonia Perovskaya and Andrei Zhelyabov are very rare. Separately and finally together, they led the lives of underground conspiracy and left no autobiographical papers. The memoirs of fellow revolutionaries who knew or glimpsed them in their shadowy activities are uniformly laudatory, written out of awe at their terrorist successes. And the police knew and recorded nothing substantial about them until much later—too late.

Since Russian male students were at first lukewarm about women's serious schooling, the first political discussion circle in which Sonia had a hand was feminine. They read and discussed controversial books and tracts. Sonia was very strict, requiring steady attendance and homework. Feminism was not the issue. "Social justice" and how to achieve it absorbed the participants.

This emphasis made it easy to accept the invitation of a male group, Chaikovsky Circle, to join forces. Before the expanded group settled down to mutual discussions, Sonia succeeded in getting a male member who was as interested in skirt-chasing as in dialectics expelled. Severe chastity was the rule in the Chaikovsky Circle matched by cohesion and benevolence in its alternative family setting. Unanimity was the desired outcome of their political discussions.

One of the early St. Petersburg communes has been described as a two-story wooden structure in which about twenty persons lived two to a room; the women upstairs, the men on the ground floor. Guests could stretch out overnight in a dining hall also used for political discussions and lecture meetings. All monies were given to the appointed housekeeper. The diet was spartan and usually meatless except when a veterinarian student procured slaughtered horse flesh. The huge tea samovar was the social center of a daily life which focused on endless discussions.

This was the life style Sonia instinctively sought, savored and soon partly commanded. It was as pure, earnest and innocent as it ever would be. At this time, 1870–71, she was content but progressing toward a radical activist future.

A thousand miles to the south Andrei Zhelyabov entered in 1869 the university at Odessa as an ex-serf who made it to law school. He is recalled as a one-suit student. And that, purchased off a second-hand rack, was too small and emphasized a tall, gangling appearance. However, poverty did not impair his popularity at the school. Dashing masculine charm, a good mind, and a happy-go-lucky demeanor carried him through many crises.

Not every crisis was related to stretching a bowl of soup into a day's sustenance. Though not yet a troublemaker, Andrei is fairly described as a trouble-seeker. He was ready to rally against constituted authority on any occasion. He would have become a revolutionary early on had there been such an organization at their provincial school. But perhaps because of inferiority feelings because of his serf origin he was not yet ready to initiate organized political activity himself. He took a hand in mild antiestablishment baiting, like teaching forbidden curricula to a group of admiring girl students.

Quick of mind, charismatic in personality, and fluent—indeed glib—of tongue, Andrei would have made an outstand-

Lambs Into Wolves

ing lawyer. As a liberal advocate he might have represented the revolutionaries in the extensive trials to come. But this was not to be because of the "Bogishich incident" in the fall of 1871.

Professor Bogishich was a visiting lecturer from Austria-Hungary, who neither understood Russian or local custom very well. Unused to and despising student informality as practiced in Odessa he became enraged one day when he saw a student lounging on his bench in class.

"Do you think you are in a tavern?" he shouted.

The student's mumbled reply was amicable, but the professor misunderstood and assumed impudence. Bogishich rushed from the podium and physically ejected the student.

Nobody showed up at the next Bogishich class. But a crowd of students stood in the corridor whistling and hissing. A university confrontation was on. A student delegation marched to the school administrator with their demands for an apology. Among the leaders, though he neither knew the student or attended Professor Bogishich's classes, was Andrei Zhelyabov!

An agreement was reached. The professor would make a mild apology at the next class. It was well attended, but this time the professor didn't show up! Feeling doubly insulted, the students demonstrated, and word of the uproar reached St. Petersburg. The mossbacked Minister of Education, Count Tolstoi (an uncle of Sonia's), was very hardnosed on student upheavals and the word came back—expel the ringleaders. This was done reluctantly by the local school authority.

Andrei's schooling ended. He tried to reenter after a year and though the Odessa administrators were willing, he was turned down on orders from St. Petersburg where a dossier on Zhelyabov had been started. The ex-university student had some experience in tutoring, and by this means, together with farm labor, Andrei patched together a living. He had learned what penalties were involved when a Russian student incurred the ill will of the tsar's bureaucracy.

Not every Russian proto-revolutionist was innocent, humane, or happy-go-lucky. There was by terrible example Sergei Nechaev, a young man who justified feelings of paranoia within the tsarist regime. This son of a serf was cruel and remorseless in his driving ambition to make and lead a bloody revolution.

By 1869, Nechaev, a teacher in St. Petersburg, was running a small revolutionary cell. He is recalled as slight in figure, threadbare in clothes, but in his dark, narrow face were the fevered eyes of a political zealot. When police attention raised the prospect of early arrests, the leader coldly decided to abandon his companions and leave Russia for a time. Nechaev was a diabolical plotter in a hurry and had no time for jail. As for his followers, he felt that imprisonment would toughen their revolutionary fervor.

His escape plan was based on deceit and the expendability of others. First he sent a note to Vera Zazulich, whom he had unsuccessfully tried to romance, saying he had been arrested and was en route to the worst tsarist prison. This was designed to install a hero/martyr image among his associates. But Nechaev had really gone to Switzerland, the paradise of Russian political exiles.

There he contacted Michael Bakunin. Bakunin was a renowned revolutionary hero of the past who, escaping Siberian exile, was now urging radical measures inside Russia from his refuge in Switzerland. Nechaev told Bakunin that he, Nechaev, was the leader of a vast underground organization in Russia and had just escaped from a tsarist prison. All that he needed to spark a thorough-going revolution was *money*.

Lambs Into Wolves

Bakunin was really out of touch with events inside Russia but unwilling to admit it. So he was taken in by his visitor, but took in Nechaev, too. Bakunin confided that he was the head of a vast revolutionary movement outside Russia and issued Nechaev certificate of membership number 2771 in the non-existent organization. Though Bakunin had no money to give Nechaev, he knew that Alexander Herzen, a prominent exile living in London, controlled a bequest to aid revolutionary activities. Nechaev went to London, lied impressively, and secured ten thousand francs.

He was about ready to return to Russia. He had continued the deception by writing the same Vera Zazulich and telling her how he had escaped prison in a general's uniform he had inveigled and was now a buddy of Bakunin and Herzen. To expand his reputation, Nechaev wrote "The Revolutionary Catechism," as cold-blooded a document on the subject as has ever been written. A few excerpts:

> *The revolutionary despises public opinion . . . for him morality is everything which contributes to the triumph of the revolution . . . He is merciless toward the state and . . . the educated classes . . . All soft and tender affections arising from kinship, friendship and love, all gratitude and even all honor must be obliterated . . . Night and day he must have but one thought, one aim—merciless destruction . . .*

Nechaev returned to Russia and started a small revolutionary cell in Moscow. He told his principal associates that he represented a national radical group whose orders, transmitted through him, must be executed exactly and that a national revolution was but a few months away. After a while, one of his companions, Ivan Ivanov, came to doubt the existence of the organization and to disagree with some of Nechaev's commands.

This was not at all in the spirit of "The Revolutionary Catechism" and Nechaev told the others of the inner circle that orders had come down from above that Ivanov must be executed for treason. The accomplices were most reluctant. But the diabolical personality of their leader overwhelmed them. Ivanov was lured to a grotto in a Moscow park where a printing press had supposedly been buried. The murderers met him there in the darkness. Ivanov resisted and was shot to death by Nechaev after strangulation failed. The body was clumsily thrown into a pond, where it was soon discovered, and the police were quickly on their trail.

Again Nechaev abandoned his companions, fleeing once more to Switzerland. In his cold, pragmatic way, he considered them a weak lot and thereby unworthy. They had talked a lot of bloodthirsty theory but had never killed anyone. The only accomplices who counted were those who would go out "and murder the government."

A great show trial was mounted in 1871 to judge the murder of Ivanov and especially to highlight the accompanying revolutionary activities. In the style of the era the police snared about three hundred persons—anyone who it could be alleged had ever had any contact with Nechaev. This group was reduced to eighty-four by trial time and the only persons convicted were the actual murder accomplices. The cold-blooded machinations of "the Nechaev monster" were thoroughly publicized, chilling conservatives and radicals alike.

In Switzerland, Nechaev fell out with his patron Bakunin, and the lurid trial publicity caused most of the other Russian

Lambs Into Wolves

exiles to shun him also. In 1872, he was picked up by the Swiss on the murder charge and turned over to the Russian police. In short order he really entered prison. The "caged tiger" was a dangerous prisoner, ever plotting escape, subverting guards, smuggling messages, but never quite succeeding in the big break before he died of scurvy in a tsarist dungeon about ten years later.

The Nechaev affair was a sensation in Russia. The writer Dostoevski, transplanted its dark fascination into his novel *The Possessed*. Conservatives were further frightened into police state hysteria, while the earnest radical movement within Russia was embarrassed and troubled. The importance of Nechaev's terrible example was that it turned off for some years any desire for centralized leadership in the radical movement.

By 1872-73, there were youth social study/action groups in all the major cities of Russia. They were modeled on the elite Chaikovsky Circle and occasionally were in contact. The Chaikovsky group was now acting upon the teachings of P. L. Lavrov, another exile bombarding the homeland with political tracts.

His message emphasized gentry guilt, a concept that appealed to the consciences of the young radicals, who with few exceptions were sons and daughters of the privileged classes. For generations, Lavrov proclaimed, their families had rested on the backs of the peasantry. The landowners were drones immorally squeezing an unearned, useless living from the sweat of the working classes. Now all this past and present guilt must be atoned for by *their* generation! They must go to the People and help them.

A two-step program was recommended. First, the young apostles must make friends with the peasantry in the country, the workers in the cities, and prove their affection by laboring beside them and using their educated intellects to improve the lives of the lower classes. Second, they must raise the political expectations of the People. They must be urged to give up their childlike dependence on the goodness of the tsar and turned into an independent political force. And in that (perhaps distant) day, Lavrov prophesied, fifty million of the People could not be denied their national inheritance and together would shape a new socialist paradise!

From the Chaikovsky Circle Sonia led the way—out of the commune and into city life, propagandizing, organizing at the university and among the workers. And with this activity launched, she made a new example in a long journey southward into the Russian heartlands, "going to the People." Here her work was in the way of person-to-person aid, using her medical skills in vaccination, midwife techniques, and personal hygiene. Existence was grim, milk and roots for food, bed of straw. But adversity would always rather suit her stoic, stubborn disposition.

The opportunity for meaningful political instruction was almost nil, but we are told that she was happiest when working in the capacity of nurse or teacher. The work of Sonia and others going from the circles to the people in 1872–1873 caused no significant political ripples. The peasantry were not at all in the mood that the activist Bakunin, isolated in Switzerland, proclaimed them to be—political tinder awaiting a revolutionist's spark.

In the fall of 1873, back in St. Petersburg, Sonia was arrested while leading a worker's demonstration and entered prison at the age of nineteen. It was a year before her father, trusting he had instilled a meaningful lesson upon his hardheaded daughter, arranged bail. The terms of release, to which she agreed and honored, confined her to the southern estate of her mother's family, where she remained isolated from political contact awaiting trial, a period the police stretched into years, until 1878.

The Russian government made a serious blunder in its student policy in 1873. It was rightly concerned that hundreds of its best and brightest young people who were studying abroad were being subverted by the radical exiles. Suddenly a decree was issued forbidding outward student travel and ordering all Russian students abroad to return to the homeland or forfeit their citizenship.

It would have been more effective for stemming dissent had the regime quarantined the outsiders in some way. As it was the students obeyed the order and brought back their radical "infection" with them, so that in the following year it expanded into an epidemic.

Stirred by the example of Sonia and others, scores of youthful apostles, earnest zealots from populist circles across Russia, planned evangelical pilgrimages for the summer of 1874. But these elite, serious populists turned out to be a minority in the vast outpouring of young people, trendy, adventurous, out on a romp.

They joined by the hundreds. It was the thing to do in June of 1874. A commentator writing within ten years of the event describes what happened:

> *Young people of both sexes forsook the parental roof or left their studies at school and university to hasten by every road, highway and river with their message of enlightenment and revolt to the country districts. In order to win over the people and make their task*

all the easier, many of these enthusiasts put on peasant's attire, gave a blowzed appearance to their faces by rubbing them with grease or steeped their hands in brine until they became as rough and hard as those of a mushik himself.

Young men who had been delicately brought up learned the trade of the blacksmith, the carpenter, the shoemaker, or the locksmith, in order to come more immediately into contact with the artisan classes; young women of the best families worked in the factories like common peasants, or took a share as agriculturists in the labors of the fields.

Well, it was all a big flop!

The political feelings of the peasants had not changed. Whatever contempt or hatred applied to local officials, the tsar was still revered as their heavenly father on earth, whose good intentions on their behalf were continually frustrated by lower rungs of authority. They dismissed revolutionary doctrines as impious and dangerous. They laughed at the city ways of their self-appointed teachers, at their clumsy attempts to blend into the barnyard. Sometimes they ended by denouncing them to the police.

The activist in the field needed to keep moving to prevent arrest, and this did no good for the effectiveness of political propagandizing. Of course, many of the young people could not take the life at all and returned to their homes. There were many disillusionments.

Some of the young gentry so overdid their peasant costuming as to be looked upon as bums to be avoided by ordinary

Lambs Into Wolves

country folk. Distributors of political leaflets learned that the illiterate peasants who welcomed their tracts used them to roll cigarettes! Many of the rustics were not saintly at all and visualized "social justice" as personally getting the upper hand and becoming as cruel and grasping as any present landlord. The attention given to political speeches was often superficial—like listening to a fairy tale.

A wise old peasant, watching an ex-medical student clumsily attempting carpentry, summed it up:

"Give it up young man! I will give you good advice: There is no better vocation than to become a doctor."

Most of the youthful apostles would have quietly yielded to this type of counsel once the high fever of populist activism had been cooled naturally by reality. But again the government blundered, tragically for all concerned:

> . . . *Success was impossible. The people were not ripe enough for a revolution. The propagandists were not mature or experienced enough to prepare for one. With a simple faith even more credulous than that of the peasants they hoped to convince, they neglected the commonest precautions, scarcely concealed their movements from the police, in some cases allowed their mission to become a matter of public notoriety. The authorities took early action against the propaganda. Hundreds were arrested and thrown into prison* . . .

"Prison" in 1874 was not an overnight bust with the prospect of easy bail in the morning. The official attitude was: Take them out of circulation and keep them out. For months or years!

Tsarist jails were not pleasant retreats; some were horrors, but on the whole they were less inhuman than the political prisons of twentieth century dictatorships. The radical student prisoners of the 1870s were nearly all from the upper classes and noticeable deference was granted by prison guards and officials alike.

One result was a good deal of personal contact among the prisoners, and in the tradition of penitentiary contacts, soft-minded amateurs were converted into tough-minded professionals —lambs into wolves. The mental therapy of planning how to get even was not always enough. For some, anger and disillusionment turned into despair:

> *Mr. Prosecutor, my dear sir, here I am thrown into this hole, positively for no reason at all: am deprived of light, air, space, and the company of people: Well —do you want me to hang myself—have you no God? Never will I believe it's the tsar's wish to have men thrown positively for nothing into such holes: Let me out, give me back light, air, and space!*

The letter drew no reply and this young man joined a grisly toll of young jail suicides.

Andrei Zhelyabov sat out the political pilgrimages. Or rather, he was already there with the People. His political situation was indefinite. Though he thought of himself as a revolutionary, his contacts with the circles were minor and off and on. In the southern cities of Odessa, Kharkov, Kiev, circle members knew vaguely about Andrei, had met him a few times, thought the slim, handsome fellow a talker without accomplishments to show.

Andrei Zhelyabov in the 1870s, before he began his populist, then terrorist activities. (Drawing published in Andrei Zhelyabov *by A. Budiak, published in the Soviet Union in 1965.)*

Probably it was a class thing. The leadership of the circles tended to be elitist, pedigreed sons and daughters of the aristocracy. Andrei felt his serf origins made him an outsider. It is known that he detested the mannerisms (a charm and charisma very like his own) of Valerian Osinski, a leader in the south. Andrei would not amount to much as a revolutionary figure until, much later, he was specifically asked to participate in terrorism.

Meanwhile, during a summer's employment as tutor at the home of a wealthy and politically liberal manufacturer, his pupil, Olga Yahnenko, fell in love with her dashing instructor. Andrei responded, and Papa agreed to a wedding. It was not a very happy marriage because of differing aims. Olga did not object to Andrei's revolutionary credo, but felt that considerations of home and family (a son was born in 1876) came first. But with Andrei, first loyalty was always to the movement, ill-defined though his contact with it was in the first years.

Trouble came when a friend was arrested in the countryside. Andrei sent a coded message to the prisoner's wife. It was intercepted, and Zhelyabov drew four months of jail time for his friendly gesture.

The years ticked by, and in 1877, the leisurely authorities decided to put on two catch-all show trials of indicted and detained radicals and summer apostles. The second and most famed was the Trial of the 193, where they led off with Sonia Perovskaya hoping that after her fallow years (she had worked as a nurse, studied medicine) with her family she would recant.

But Sonia turned tables on the court, refusing to accept their authority amid impassioned political commentary. Other prisoners did the same. Nearly all, including Perovskaya, were acquitted! The trial—jokingly called a government-sponsored convention of radicals—was a public relations disaster for the regime.

Among others acquitted was Andrei Zhelyabov, who had been recalled because of the coded letter affair. So Andrei and Sonia met for the first time in the courtroom. He was impressed with the diminutive, blue-eyed blonde; the famed, formidable la Perovskaya. But Sonia did not respond at all . . . just another *man*.

At the end of the trials the hardened veterans of four to ten years of radical dissent took stock. They had failed to generate popular revolution by exhortation, and the police had shown a determination to wipe them out by harassment and imprisonment. It was time to reconsider Chernyshevsky's eternal question—*What Is to Be Done?* And suddenly an alternative presented itself. Not the stuff of foreign-based heavy thinkers, rather a heroic deed perfectly performed by a determined young woman. The Trepov affair became a hinge of the future.

General Feodor Trepov was the hated and feared chief of police of St. Petersburg. Gross, insulting, vain and pompous, he cared little about his public image. He did the will of his masters and had recently been rewarded with promotion to governor of the city.

One day in July, 1877, at the principal prison, the bad-tempered general encountered in the exercise yard a prisoner who did not respectfully doff his cap in Trepov's presence. Enraged, the official knocked the cap off with a sweep of his hand and ordered the prisoner to be flogged with birch rods. Many political prisoners in cells ringing the courtyard witnessed the incident and reacted by starting a prison riot.

Flogging had been a standard punishment in Russia for centuries—but as applied to serfs and others of the lower classes.

A romanticized portrait of Vera Zazulich, who was tried but acquitted for her attempt to kill General Trepov. (Sketch published in The Graphic, *May 4, 1878.)*

Lambs Into Wolves

Daring to beat an *intelligent!*—that is a member of the gentry—combined with Trepov's villainous image incited the riot and caused radicals all over the country to sizzle with outrage. One who vowed to do something about it was that same Vera Zazulich who had been Nechaev's duped correspondent.

With deliberate patience Vera awaited the end of the Trial of the 193. She did not wish to prejudice their sentences. But on the day following, she was among citizens waiting to plead with the governor on personal civic matters. When he approached, Zazulich drew out from her purse a small pistol and shot him once in the side. Trepov fell to the floor while Vera dropped the pistol and stoically awaited arrest.

Well, it being an open and shut case of attempted murder—for Trepov did recover—the authorities decided to try Zazulich for that offense and soft-pedal the political side. But the prosecutor was inept while the defense attorney was brilliant. The latter turned the trial into an inquisition into the affairs of the hated Trepov. A scandal surfaced when the wounded villain, fearing he would not survive, urgently ordered his will prepared. It included monies that must have been fraudulently obtained in office.

Russian emotion overcame the law as the jury and judge dared to acquit Vera Zazulich! The outraged police awaited her exit from the courthouse to rearrest her on political charges. But the crowd surged about her protectively and in the confusion Vera escaped and was soon out of the country with her reputation made for life.

The Trepov affair made a sensational impact on the revolutionary movement. Perhaps . . . perhaps there was a short cut to power! As Andrei Zhelyabov would later remark:

"History moves too slowly—it needs a push."

III
THE TURN TOWARD TERRORISM

After the mild results of the Trial of the 193 as well as that of Vera Zazulich, there were fateful reunions and great joy in the radical circles of St. Petersburg and other cities. The toughened former inmates of the tsar's prisons settled into the populist underground resolved to plot new strategies against the government. Meanwhile Alexander II and his advisers attempted to soften the outrage at their recent public defeats by planning a massive, ruthless offensive against the tiny but pesky faction of revolutionary conspirators. From here onward to the climax, when the leadership of both sides would be annihilated, there was unrelenting back street and underground warfare.

The majority of the educated middle and upper classes stepped aside from this battle between extremists of the right and left and this cop-out allowed the conflict to become more unreasoning and final. The liberal element of this majority saw

The Turn Toward Terrorism

that with the present tension, the government would not tolerate their hopes of gradual democratization. But though they were dismayed by the rigidity of Alexander II, they could not, as good Russians, go along with a revolution. So they relapsed into neutral spectators of the war between the tsar and the revolutionists.

The government moved to improve its attack in two ways: The investigative "Third Section" of the tsar's police was enlarged and given ruthless authority to act. Hundreds of police agents were set on the trails, real or supposed, of the revolutionists. As in the past, a principal result would be the hassling or detention of hundreds of people whose connection with revolutionary conspiracy was minor or hearsay. There was no relief in the courts. These were now completely in line with police policy and became in effect its disciplinary branch.

But it was easier to recruit police agents and enlarge that bureaucracy than to hunt down real radicals. For a long time the government struggled inefficiently. Besides their own clumsiness, the regime was faced for the first time with the formation of effective, even sophisticated, underground organizations. No longer could it sweep up wide-eyed naive idealists; the radical underground had toughened and become professional.

By 1878, the idea of the study-oriented circles was far out of date. Sonia Perovskaya and others had moved from theory to action in the "Go to the People" mission experience. But this effort had failed completely before and was failing again this year. Realists among the radicals were planning a new turn of policy and tactics. Three such thinkers and doers were Alexander Mikhailov, Nikolai Morozov, and Lev Tikhomirov.

They were members of Land and Liberty, the principal St. Petersburg populist organization, and would soon form its Death

Alexander II took a tougher stance against the nihilists, sending many to prison in Siberia. In this sketch, the fortress/prison of Sts. Peter and Paul can be seen across the river. (Sketch published in The Graphic, *November 8, 1879.)*

The Turn Toward Terrorism

or Freedom faction, which evolved into the leading terrorist group. Together they turned Land and Liberty from a fellowship working with the People to a direct opponent of the tsarist regime. Not since Nechaev had there been men who so fulfilled the tsar's fears of revolutionists. In a sense it was self-fulfilled prophecy for it was the monarch's harsh policies that had hardened them over years from innocent reformers into desperate conspirators against the state.

Tikhomirov was the thinker who shifted the focus toward direct political revolution goals; Morozov was their publicist and a staunch proponent of terrorism as a tactic; Mikhailov, though, was the keystone of the organization because he emphasized and enforced security and a discipline not previously known or wanted by the young radicals.

No longer did the surviving members publicly flaunt their counterculture beliefs. They faded into a shadowy underground, anonymous hit-and-run operatives shielded in darkness. Before long Mikhailov had recruited two significant members into Land and Liberty—a clerk who worked for a Third Section administrator dealing with police spies and organizing raids on radical cells; and an engineering school dropout who was fascinated with the ways to use dynamite.

But the majority of Land and Liberty members still preferred social actions—working with the People in the countryside—and repudiated terrorism. So Mikhailov and friends waited for the right time to begin their activities. Outside, though, the war with the tsar was becoming bloodier.

In the more volatile south, a police raid on a radical printing press was met by bullets. Russian police up to that time (but not thereafter) were unarmed, and so an army unit had to be summoned. The ringleader, Kovalsky, was soon harshly sen-

Police raiding the printing press for the nihilist paper, The National Will, met with armed resistance. (Sketch published in L'Illustration, February 21, 1881.)

tenced and shot. Not long after, through coincidental timing, a mighty retaliation occurred in the north. Serge Kravchinsky duplicated Vera Zazulich's heroism and became a revolutionary star by stabbing to death (while Land and Liberty's Mikhailov observed from a distance) the chief of the hated Third Section, General Mezentsev, as he strolled on a main street of the capital. The assassin escaped handily in a buggy drawn by a racehorse.

This action was justified in the revolutionary press as a "Death for a Death." Kravchinsky soon left Russia forever, becoming, as "Stepniak," a well-known interpreter to the West of revolutionary activities. Meanwhile cynics remarked that Mezentsev was a poorly chosen target since he was known to be a most inefficient chief of the tsarist police.

Flamboyant terrorist actions continued in the south where the radicals were not controlled by party discipline. The leading spirit was Valerian Osinski, a dandy with aristocratic charm, an exotic firebrand seeking immediate fame via terrorism. He had been encouraged to go down to Kiev in the south by the ever practical Mikhailov, who was willing to see how well terrorism worked for a willing compatriot. It would be a kind of laboratory experiment. Osinski lasted about a year before arrest and execution.

His bloody deeds began with the execution of a police spy detected in the movement. Osinski next personally made a hit-and-run attack by night on a state prosecutor and returned boasting of murder. In the morning, though, he was chagrined to learn that not one of his revolver shots had found its mark.

Osinski, with bravado, selected as the next target Kiev's police chief Baron Heyking. He was another inefficient official, who additionally was inclined to be lax with the local radical faction. However Osinski reasoned that Heyking was the most

The Turn Toward Terrorism

prominent local representative of the regime and his death would bring the killers lots of publicity. A plan was devised to stab him to death and Osinski appointed one of his associates to execute the deed. He succeeded.

This was a fateful event, because the replacement, Colonel Sudeykin, was super-efficient. He rose to national prominence as one of the most skilled police executives in the art of infiltration of radical organizations. Though Osinski also planned the successful assassination of Prince Dmitri Kropotkin, Governor of Kharkov province, he and others of the Kiev leadership became victims of Colonel Sudeykin's efficiency and ended on the gallows.

In addition to scattered tactics of terror aimed at disorganization of the regime and self-publicity, the radical organizations did not forget their imprisoned fellows. Much imagination and effort was expended, sometimes successfully, on attempts to free them.

Prince Peter Kropotkin, of that same prominent family as the assassinated Kharkov governor, had early entered the radical ranks and suffered imprisonment. He became ill with scurvy and, because of his aristocratic lineage, was transferred to a relatively lightly guarded military hospital on the edge of St. Petersburg. Guards there, as elsewhere, could be easily bought off for message purposes, and soon there was active plotting with comrades outside to free him. A system of signals was devised which at times employed a red balloon (which failed to fly when needed) and a street violinist with a coded repertoire.

After several failed plots, the prince, during an exercise period, sprinted on cue of the violinist's mazurka out the hospital gate and boarded a carriage drawn by the swift horse later to be used in the Mezentsev assassination. The chase by the guards was impeded because Kropotkin's saviors had hired all available horse cabs at the scene and driven off. The jubilant escapee's first stop was at a relative's home for a change of costume, then to a barber shop to have his beard shorn. With a flourish, Kropotkin and friends decided to visit a fine St. Petersburg restaurant, where in a private room a gala reunion was held while the police vainly sought him in the back alleys of the city.

Another escape saga, again with a quality of Russian spirit to it, occurred in the south. Osinski was the planner and Michael Frolenko the performer who began by securing a job as a guard in the prison where three local revolutionary leaders were held for having incited a (failed) local peasant's revolt. The complaints about Frolenko's strictness from inmates who were in on the plot resulted in his rapid promotion. Soon the radical was assistant to the warden. The warden, though incorruptible, had a passion for vodka. So Osinski and company concocted a bogus offer to him to assume the managership of a provincial distillery. The official accepted, and Frolenko became the new prison warden and soon arranged the prisoners' escape.

Also in the south an escape plot was arranged by Sonia Perovskaya to free a comrade, Myshkin, who was one of the few of the 193 still in prison. Sonia learned that Myshkin was being transferred to another jail and laid out a plan to intercept him en route. The prisoner's party was overtaken in the countryside by horsemen in police uniforms with fake orders to receive the captive.

But either the paper was not well done or the conversation about it inept, for the prison guards became suspicious. A nervous radical set off his pistol accidentally and the bullet nipped the ear of one of the team pulling the prison carriage. The horses panicked and galloped off, dragging the buggy of the prison

The Turn Toward Terrorism

party in a desperate chase reaching the next guard station ahead of the pursuers. The failed rescuers reported shamefaced to Perovskaya, who was disdainfully furious. Just like a man to botch it!

Sonia had become a fugitive despite her acquittal by the court, for she was one of those considered a continuing danger to the state and therefore to be exiled to a provincial city where her activities could be checked. For some time the young woman had eluded the authorities, but she was eventually taken while attempting a secret visit to her mother at the family estate.

The place selected for her exile was Archangel province in the arctic north of European Russia. According to revolutionary lore, Sonia made no attempt to escape during the long train ride up to St. Petersburg because the guards were so nice. She did not want to get them into trouble. But north of the capital the second pair were more brutish and/or opportunity was better.

The trio had to pass long nighttime hours between trains at a country station and took over a small room in the depot. One guard lounged at the doorway and the other by the window. When both had lapsed into deep sleep, Sonia stepped over the entrance guard, quietly pushing the door, which fortunately opened outwards. She hid shivering in the trackside forest until the arrival of a southbound train. Though she had no ticket, she beguiled the conductor as a naïve peasant girl who didn't know you had to pay to ride. Though an aristocrat, Sonia had a gift for communication with ordinary folk and in this case used it to get a ride back to St. Petersburg.

She was welcomed by friends in the capital, where she kept her reputation as one of the icon-like founders of the movement. She met proud Serge Kravchinsky not long after his killing of Mezentsev and enjoyed a night out at the opera with the cream of revolutionary society. But after a few days Sonia made preparations to return to the south. The missionary, social uplift work of populism still attracted her more than the radicals' new preference for terrorism as a short-cut tactic.

By 1879, the movement's progress was stalled as it "either beat vainly against inertia, or met with furious persecution." Beyond the continuing toll of imprisonments and exiles to Siberia, radical casualties in the last six months of 1878 were eighteen by execution for political activities against the state. It was in this situation of mounting frustration and a building desire for vengeance that the Death and Freedom faction was able to introduce terrorism into official Land and Liberty policy.

Lev Tikhomirov, a studious priest's son, was the principal visionary planner, whose thinking, enlarged by the aggressive publicist Morozov, shifted the radicals' focus away from "the People" and toward direct overthrow of the regime and its replacement by . . . well . . . people like themselves. A popular democracy in Russia was not a looked-for end. The radicals had already learned that, left to themselves, the People would probably vote for the wrong things. If terrorism could clear the way to sudden, complete destabilization of the government, then it was the right means. These views, even in 1878, were too extreme for most of the pure populists.

Lev Tikhomirov came to Land and Liberty from the prison melting pot of the 193 and in that earlier time had become the first romantic interest in Sonia Perovskaya's life. They had once planned to marry, but she was too strong, he realized, and Lev backed out of the arrangement. Doubtless thinking of Sonia, he characterized the ladies in the movement as:

The Turn Toward Terrorism

Typical women! Not very smart, but what fanaticism, self-assurance and willpower, the latter to be sure in its lowest denominator: obstinacy. *Something will get into their heads and you will not dig it out with a scalpel.*

Lev afterward married someone else and reported in his memoirs that Sonia was "insulted and furious" but that she looked at him "with new eyes" of respect thereafter.

In the Land and Liberty organization Tikhomirov was left solely to planning. He was not considered businesslike enough to carry out the organization's secret day-to-day activities. For that, they had the practical, nuts-and-bolts Alexander Mikhailov on hand. They called him "the Janitor," a man who reliably saw to daily chores and security as well as recruiting bomb-makers and spies within the tsar's police. Yes, and he was indispensible in neatly arranging an assassination on cue. Yet, beneath the no-nonsense role, Alex had an introspective side.

One of those whose dedication to the movement was saintly in quality, Alex's personality was shaped by deep ascetic, religious attitudes. He was monkish in devotion to the radical gospel. He turned aside all sexual and most social contacts in his quest for revolutionary purism. Perhaps to compensate for denied human needs, he reveled in the fellowship of working closely with others for dangerous conspiratorial objectives. There was fascination, too, in a premonition of death just down the road. "We can do anything," Mikhailov said, "if we are not afraid to die." This was his dark credo, and the secret preparation for terroristic acts excited him as comradely high communion before approaching capture and execution.

So when Leon Mirski, a brash nineteen-year-old son of the Polish nobility, decided to find fame in radical causes, he sought out "the Janitor" for advice and aid. Mikhailov approved in principle of Mirski's plan to kill General Drenteln, the present chief of the Third Section, so he made no objection beside caution. Mirski was a dandy, a vainglorious type like Osinski, but without his cunning or luck. A principal reason for the assassination attempt was to impress a girlfriend.

Securing a superior horse and having dressed to excess in aristocratic finery, Mirski overtook Drenteln's coach on a city street and fired a pistol at the official through its glass window. Both shots were ineffective, and Mirski was unable to follow up because his high-spirited horse ran away with him, bucking and plunging until the rider was dumped into the street near a gaping policeman.

With aristocratic finesse Mirski gave orders something like this:

"See here, my good man, hold my horse while I go next door and get cleaned up."

The cop was still minding the horse when General Drenteln drove up. The cop assured the general that the young gentleman had not been injured in his fall!

So Mirski got away for then, but it was not his nature to keep his adventure to himself. His careless boastings soon brought on arrest and a sentence of death. "Watch me swing!" he bragged in an ultra-tough stance. But on reflection, he wrote very humble petitions of regret to Alexander II and was let out of the death penalty—while on the gallows platform—into life imprisonment because of his contrition and tender age. His former target, Drenteln, directed he become the cellmate of Nechaev in the

The Turn Toward Terrorism

hope Mirski would turn informer, and there is some evidence this did occur.

The thoughts of the would-be or accomplished terrorists turned toward the top. Simultaneously three different radicals approached Mikhailov proclaiming their intention of going after "the Bear," that is, the tsar, himself. They were Gregory Goldenberg, the successful assassin of Governor Kropotkin; Louis Kobilyanski, a Pole with terrorist credentials; and Alexander Soloviev, a longtime but now disgruntled rural populist, who had only fanatic resolve to offer.

The Janitor talked it over with his like-minded colleagues and they agreed to strike out Goldenberg and Kobilyanski on ethnic grounds. A pure Russian in their definition should kill the tsar, not a Jew or a Pole. Also the assassination of Alexander II ought to have organization support so it could take the credit for it afterward. So a meeting of the Land and Liberty membership in town was called to consider the matter.

The radicals were flush enough at this time to hire a room for their climactic meeting. Soloviev was not there, nor did Mikhailov identify the assassination candidate. But the proposal to raise terrorism in the highest degree to the policy of Land and Liberty provoked a storm of protest from the populist moderates present and in majority.

Insanity! Stupidity! They couldn't believe their ears! One member hinted he would warn the monarch. Another, opposing him, said he would kill him if he did! Amid the uproar and threatened brawl there came a portentous pounding on the door.

Mikhailov reasserted control, "The police! Are we going to defend ourselves?"

Reunited, they swore to resist. But it was only the porter who had been roused by the shouting.

So without organization support the Janitor privately provided Soloviev with poison and revolver. The earnest terrorist practiced shooting daily. But he was a naive, untried instrument, as Mikhailov, as a detached observer, surely reckoned. Probably this was excused because the Janitor knew from observation that the tsar would likely be an easy target.

Every morning Alexander II went out into the parkland near the Winter Palace for a brisk walk. The area was open to public strollers too, but the monarch was not closely guarded. His pride did not allow this, so that though security personnel were in the area, he was alone when he came face to face with Alexander Soloviev on the morning of April 2, 1879.

As Soloviev pulled out his revolver, the emperor shouted in distress to a building guard, but the soldier only snapped to attention. The terrorist opened fire as the Tsar retreated and, agile for his age, hop-scotched evasively, bending and dipping as five bullets whizzed past. He eventually fell to the ground unscathed but for a bullet hole in his clothing.

Soloviev turned and ran. It is reported that the first person to intercept him was a pedestrian, a sturdy milkmaid. As he swallowed the poison he was captured by police and an emetic was soon administered so that he survived. Thus ended the third assassination attempt on Alexander II.

Mikhailov the terrorist "coach" was again looking on from the sideline. The Janitor's evaluation of his gang that couldn't shoot straight was final: No more guns—in the future, bombs!

The next day General Drenteln the police boss received a letter threatening his life anew if Soloviev was tortured. It was signed "The Executive Committee" and carried a symbol of

A third unsuccessful attempt on the tsar's life was made by Alexander Soloviev. The French magazine, L'Illustration, published this inaccurate rendering of Soloviev, the nihilist who couldn't shoot straight.

crossed hatchet, knife, and pistol. The Third Section had noted this seal before; they had seen it as a marker left with the bodies of executed police spies.

A nonexistent "Executive Committee" had been the idea of Osinski, borrowed from Nechaev's idea of raising the fear of "them" through promoting imaginary organizations of fantastic size and importance. There would soon be a real and potent Executive Committee, but in this case Mikhailov was just carrying on Osinski's ploy.

Whether the warning was heeded or not, Soloviev appears to have revealed nothing of his terrorist connections. In May he was hanged before a crowd of eighty thousand. The government now divided the nation into military districts under permanent martial law with one-way processing courts to deal harshly with suspects.

It was becoming impossible to act as a propagandist for the People, and leaders of that faction blamed terrorists' acts for the pressure. The terrorists replied that theirs was the only course left open by the government's counterterror. So it was agreed that a national convention of radicals must occur to thrash out the matter.

Mikhailov, Tikhomirov and friends saw this conference as a make-or-break affair for obtaining a party consent for terrorism. But they worried they would be too few and looked abroad into provincial Russia for likely recruits. Michael Frolenko, the former Kiev "prison warden," put forth the name of Andrei Zhelyabov.

There was skepticism—he was only a talker. He'd said some of the right things, as in his rejection of the populist faction: "Like fish beating their heads against the ice." But where had he been in the last year when radical revolutionist activities

The execution of Soloviev as depicted in L'Illustration *of June 28, 1879.*

fermented in the south? Tending his cabbage patch like any peasant! Well, temporized Frolenko, you see he couldn't stand Osinski.

Mikhailov pondered the suggestion. He was making a trip down to Odessa soon and could take the opportunity to interview Zhelyabov, who lived in the nearby countryside. But the main purpose of the trip south was organization financing.

Money—where did the radicals get theirs? There seems to have always been enough of it. It came in as family remittances to lost sons and daughters and as conscience money from those who approved of the movement but would not risk their own necks in its service, and as contributions from exiles and sympathizers abroad. More dramatically there was in this period a bank robbery or two. There were also several wealthy followers who made their fortunes (inheritances) available to the radicals.

The Janitor went south in pursuit of a small fortune willed to the organization by Dmitri Lizogub, a saintly, impractical, but generous believer in the radical cause. He was now in prison and would soon be hanged for little more than guilt by association. Although his money manager had been instructed to turn over Lizogub's estate to Land and Liberty, the executor was wavering. Indeed, by the time Mikhailov arrived, a police trap had been set with the manager's assistance, which the wily revolutionist barely avoided.

No money; but the Janitor pragmatically went on to see Zhelyabov. He spoke frankly: Terrorism was the way to radical goals and the emperor was its principal target. Would Andrei come in directly to that mission?

Here was the fateful decision of a lifetime. Should he go north to possible bloody triumph and probable death? Or remain

The Turn Toward Terrorism

a committed family man on the sideline, a safe but futile talker in the cabbage field?

Andrei's reply was conditional. Yes, he agreed that the nation would be relieved of a terrible despot if Alexander II was killed, and he was willing to take a hand in achieving it. But he had family responsibilities, too. Zhelyabov stated he would participate in one assassination attempt and then return to his family living here on the farm. Mikhailov was impressed with this prospective terrorist and agreed to Andrei's restrictions. Unknowing, the Janitor had recruited his successor.

Soon afterward Andrei realized that the pull upon him toward the dark side of revolutionary activity was overwhelming and exclusive. He could not, would not ever return to his former life. So, painfully, he told his wife of his decision and urged her to obtain a divorce. She however, still loving him and hoping for his eventual return, refused. Andrei parted from wife and son and went north to his bloody destiny.

The Death or Freedom faction had chosen for their strategy meeting a hot springs resort, Lipetsk. The police were unaware of their presence in this unlikely revolutionary locale. It was at Lipetsk that Andrei Zhelyabov made a head-turning introductory appearance. The others were impressed favorably. Tall and handsome and in fine physical condition from steady farm labor, Andrei, in a feat of strength, burst the skin of his palms lifting the corner of a wagon containing two peasants a few inches off the ground.

Andrei was also strong in the head, arguing powerfully in a speech that because the regime offered no freedoms and no quarter to the radicals, they were justified in following any means and taking up any weapons they could find. And they should aim for the top man, the tsar, who appointed and supported the cruel regional military governors. The pent-up revolutionary sentiments stewing in him for a decade gushed out. He was a talker all right and brimming with charm as well. By the end of the first day at Lipetsk he was more than a member. Zhelyabov was already a leader.

But a leader in a very small organization—there were just eleven people at the Lipetsk meeting. In spite of this, they would achieve a nightmare notoriety within the tsarist circles far out of proportion to their numbers. It was at Lipetsk that the real and deadly Executive Committee was founded as a strict and supersecret terrorist fellowship. Publicly, Mikhailov and his comrades, including Zhelyabov, always denied membership and claimed to be only low-level servants of that mysterious and extremely powerful organization. The Executive Committee formally sentenced Alexander II to death at its hands and moved on to the main radical conference in the provincial town of Voronezh.

The addition there of active rural populists raised the attendance to twenty-one persons. At several picnic-like meetings in parks and woodlands, this tiny fanatical political fragment argued over how to topple an empire. Again Zhelyabov was a principal speaker on behalf of terrorist tactics to force the regime into such concessions as constitutional government. A good and pure populist government including the People would have to wait.

Andrei and his associates were persuasive and prevailed. Georgy Plekhanov, the populist leader, walked out of the gathering in frustration. Recalling that the imperial heir was also named Alexander, Plekhanov said that killing the tsar

The Turn Toward Terrorism

would result in placing a "III" after the name of Alexander, nothing more. Nevertheless, it was agreed to include terrorism in Land and Liberty activities and to allot one third of available funds for that purpose.

Sonia Perovskaya came as a populist delegate to Voronezh.

Sonia Perovskaya in the late 1870s, when she turned from populism to terrorism. (From Sofia Perovskaya *by Elena Segal, published in the Soviet Union in 1962.)*

The veteran radical made it plain that she was quite miffed that an invitation to Lipetsk had not also been given. But she had remained slow to accept terrorism as a principal tool, and that was why she had been passed over by Mikhailov and Tikhomirov. At Voronezh, Sonia clashed repeatedly with Zhelyabov over his rejection of pure populist ideals. But Sonia was an activist before all else, and when the turn toward terrorism became a fact, she willingly joined the most zealous faction and soon became a member of the Executive Committee itself.

The compromise struck at Voronezh soon expired. Land and Liberty split into "The People's Will" (terrorist agenda) and "The Black Repartition" (agrarian reform, namely the partition to the peasants of fertile black soil lands). The People's Will (Executive Committee) now set out "to annihilate the most harmful officials" and thereby "undermine conviction in the strength of the regime." When the People realized it was possible to successfully fight the government then, the radicals theorized, the revolution would surely occur with The People's Will leading the charge.

The most "harmful official" was winding up his summer's sojourn on his Crimean royal estate and preparing to return to St. Petersburg. The People's Will vowed that Alexander II would not come back alive. The Janitor's plans were well advanced. It would be all over for the tsar in the flash of a bomb blast!

IV

THE SIEGE OF THE WINTER PALACE

Dynamite had been invented in 1866 by Alfred Nobel (who compensated by creating the humanitarian Nobel Prizes), but it was not readily available in Russia. However Mikhailov, the Janitor, had recruited into The People's Will Nikolai Kibalchich, a whiz kid of explosive chemistry. The studious engineering student, a nonpolitical drudge at the time, had been jerked around by the police and imprisoned for three years for merely taking temporary custody of a packet of revolutionary propaganda. He came out of jail a violent opponent of the tsar and devoted the remainder of his short life to constructing for the Executive Committee the bombs designed for Alexander II's destruction.

On paper, the planning for the tsar's murder was extraordinarily thorough. Normally the route of the monarch's journey to his capital would be by sea from his Crimean estate to the port of Odessa, then by rail northward via Moscow to St. Petersburg. Therefore the first explosive was to be installed under the rail line near Odessa. Another charge would be placed at Alexanderovsk in the south on the single rail line northward. Finally still another dynamite bomb would be buried beneath the rails on the southern approach to Moscow. Alexander II was not expected to survive this triple-threat gauntlet run.

Vera Figner, the lady revolutionist with the most aristocratic bearing and connections, went down to Odessa lugging a suitcase stuffed with dynamite. She arranged an appointment with a high rail official to beg for a watchman job for an ailing servant. Though Ms. Figner complained of the official's aggressive amorous attention she secured the favor. The "servant" Michael Frolenko and "wife" Tatiana Lebedeva prepared to tunnel beneath the rail line from their trackside watchman's hut.

But the weather was particularly perverse that late Russian fall and Alexander II, who suffered from asthma and feared seasickness, decided to journey entirely by rail on a route that bypassed Odessa. The dynamite that had been brought south remained unused as the Odessa option was cancelled out.

The weather was a nasty factor at the Alexanderovsk site also. Andrei Zhelyabov and "wife" Anna Yakimova installed themselves in the small town as a merchant couple planning to invest capital in a tannery enterprise. So by day they acted their roles at business and social levels while by night Andrei and two helpers recruited from contacts in Kharkov went out to mine the railroad from a culvert at a point where an explosion would hurl the train down a seventy-five foot embankment. It rained and rained, and each day they feared it would change to snow, rendering work impossible due to the footprints they would leave behind in the snow cover.

The Siege of the Winter Palace

The snow did not come but it was a soggy, sloppy, haphazard job performed mainly by Zhelyabov while his companions watched for frequent railway patrols. Finally, after many nights of hiding or scrambling in the frigid mud, one of the two brass cylinders of dynamite was in place. On an especially sodden night the other slithered out of Zhelyabov's grasp, down out of sight into a stagnant pool. Andrei waded into the icy water and by brute strength wrestled out the slippery engine of destruction.

Working all day at public relations and most of the night with the diabolical devices took its toll on the strong Zhelyabov. He had screaming nightmares and came down with the flu. Word came from a confederate of the imperial train's schedule. The terrorists struggled and completed the wiring for detonation by dawn of the fateful day.

Alexander II and entourage traveled in three trains. There had been vague but somber rumors that some mischief would occur en route, and it is said that the train crews wore clean shirts—a doleful tribute to the superstition that it was best to meet death in fresh clothing. It was reported to the conspirators that the tsar was aboard the fourth coach of the second train.

So it was that at about ten o'clock on the morning of November 18, 1879, three terrorists sat dripping under a steady rain in their horse-drawn cart at trackside. If not killed or maimed by debris from the wreck they still would have little chance to escape out there in the open, flat Russian steppe. But Zhelyabov had become a true revolutionary fanatic of the Executive Committee, whose death wish nearly matched that of Mikhailov's, and his young helpers were mesmerized by his commanding personality.

The first train appeared and rolled swiftly by. After a few minutes they heard and saw the second train rushing by overhead. Zhelyabov firmly and precisely joined the detonating wires—and cursing tried again and again.

No explosion—not even a pop!

After the third train had passed, the trio glumly inspected their handiwork, but could not detect the malfunction. Then a severe lassitude of exhaustion and depression overtook Zhelyabov. Later that day the rain changed to snow and the bomb site whitened. The dynamite charges would have to be abandoned for now. Meanwhile at a small house near the railroad track outside of Moscow an urgent telegram arrived:

PRICE OF FLOUR TWO RUBLES. OUR PRICE FOUR.

This naive cryptography signified second train, fourth car.

The Moscow operation was the largest of the terrorist dynamite traps set along the tsar's perilous route to St. Petersburg. Probably this was because the Janitor took a personal hand in it as did nearly all of the Executive Committee. A small house was purchased in a sparsely settled outskirt of Moscow, an area of market gardens and land fills. The house was about one hundred fifty feet from the main rail line, close enough to dig a tunnel to blow up the tsar, but far enough away to allow them to survive the blast and perhaps escape.

The tenants of the dwelling were evicted by its new owners, a worker couple Lev Hartmann and "wife" Sonia Perovskaya. This was Sonia's first terrorist outing for the Executive Committee, which offered it to her though she was not yet formally aligned to it. Sonia, craving real action, abandoned her propaganda activities to join in the attempt. Hartmann, a relatively new member of the committee, was chosen because he had

The house outside Moscow from which the Executive Committee attempted to blow up the tsar's railway car. (Sketch published in The Graphic, *December 20, 1879.)*

manual skills and experience, a rarity among the sons of the middle and upper classes.

The digging brigade lodged in the city and arrived in pre-dawn darkness to labor until about ten o'clock in the evening. They needed frequent rest breaks and a big meal at two o'clock in the afternoon. But anyone calling at the house by the track in daylight would find only Sonia on hand. The tunnelers would have been warned by a signaling device and be still until the visitor departed.

Interruptions and minor alarms were frequent, for sparse settlement did not mean they had no neighbors or that the neighbors were not normally nosy about the new couple. In the event of a police raid there was installed in the house a vial of nitroglycerine and Perovskaya possessed a pistol to fire into it with effect of blowing everyone and everything to bits. This security to the ultimate degree bore the imprint of Mikhailov.

Sonia, from long experience in populist activity, knew exactly how to act like a working class wife of country origin and what to expect and turn back to the simple inhabitants of the locality.

When neighbors wondered out loud, why such large quantities of food came into the house, Sonia blamed it on their cat. She described it as a ravenous monster with the devil's appetite and then some! And her husband, too; he had an unbelievable appetite.

One day the former tenant came by seeking a forgotten pot of jam left in the *basement*. Sonia handled this emergency by fidgeting and fussing about before confessing she'd misplaced the cellar key. She promised to bring the jam around later and followed through on this.

There was a real crisis when a fire broke out in a wooden

The Siege of the Winter Palace

structure and the neighbors came running to help put it out. Sonia ran to meet them waving a sacred icon image over her head. Let God's will be done, she told them. And these devout folk understood the idea that since God started the fire He will put it out if that were to be. Inside her comrades covertly assisted "God" in successfully dousing the flames.

In the basement no one knew much about tunneling. They had a short spade for chipping at the earth face and two shovels for moving it back; also, later, a crude tow box. The lengthening hole was three and a half feet high, two and a half feet wide, shored up by a triangular brace of boards. Guided by compass the burrowers proceeded at about one foot per hour. But many, many hours were expended in coping with the difficulties and perils of tunneling itself.

As the narrow passage lengthened ventilation became poorer, making for short work periods and claustrophobia. It rained at Moscow too and the tunnel became water soaked. A depression appeared in a cart track where it ran over the tunnel, which needed hasty repair. The closer they approached the rails, the more the ground shook when a train passed, raising fears of cave-in and trapped suffocation. Several diggers carried poison to quicken such an end. Dirt disposal, though always a severe problem for secret tunnelers, was a little easier in their semi-rural surroundings.

Reactions differed among the Executive Committee miners. The bloodthirsty Morozov found he could not abide the confined closeness of the earthen walls and had to quit. The Janitor, however, didn't flinch, and as a man always anticipating death awaited it calmly when the ground vibrated and roared around him as a train rumbled by a few feet above.

Another man who couldn't take it in the tunnel was Gregory

Goldenberg. But he was the odd man in the committee in spite of being a founding member. He had come to them with the credential of having singlehandedly stalked and killed Governor Kropotkin, so they had had to take him on. Highly excitable and subject to the contrasting moods typical of a manic-depressive, he was probably mentally ill and should not have been a conspirator.

Goldenberg turned up at Alexanderovsk, but Zhelyabov didn't want him and sent him on to Moscow with advice that they always needed diggers there. Now the Moscow conspirators devised a plan to be temporarily rid of their wobbly fifth wheel. Their explosives specialist believed that the supply of dynamite on hand was possibly not sufficient. They had encountered a mass of large stones below the rail bed itself. There was no more explosive currently available from their own factory, but there was the unused stock down at Odessa, and they dispatched Gregory Goldenberg to fetch it.

The stony rail bed presented another difficulty. The rocks were very difficult to remove in the cramped tunnel and there was the risk of the rails sinking, which would surely draw fatal attention. A sophisticated drill was needed, but they had not the rubles to buy it. So they mortgaged the house! Loans for lower-class householders was a reform of Alexander II.

This brought on another crisis for Perovskaya to face up to. A loan inspector came to look over the property. Sonia shifted easily into a pose of stubborn, thick-headed resolve in refusing to admit him, saying over and over that no one could enter the house when the master was not at home. The official gave up and went away and never bothered to return.

The tunnel was finished in time and the explosive charge set. It was the original quantity, for Goldenberg had not returned

Perovskaya and Shiraev blew up the train precisely on schedule —but it was the wrong train! (Sketch published in The Graphic, *December 20, 1879.)*

from the south. According to Hartmann who went abroad and long survived, they had a victory party on the afternoon of November 19. They sat around a table stagily set with eight daggers stuck into its surface above eight revolvers. Vodka flowed as they sang revolutionary songs ending with the "Marseillaise."

Then everyone departed except Perovskaya and Stepan Shiraev the explosives man. Sonia was entrusted with signaling from above to her colleague in the basement the exact moment for the explosive. At about ten o'clock that evening a brightly lighted train passed and at ten-twenty-five another approached. Perovskaya signaled precisely and Shiraev followed through.

With the sharp blast the fourth coach heaved and burst as it rolled over at trackside. The landscape was splattered with crimson goo. Royal blood? No, the Tsar's favorite jam from his estate. It was the wrong train—Alexander II was safe inside the Kremlin! An official leaped from the disabled train and, smelling dynamite, peered closely at the house by the track where "a light was burning in front of the icon, the samovar was boiling, and the tea things were on the table," but no one was visible.

The bombed train carried the imperial baggage and no one was killed. This unit had been in the lead but slowing because of its excessive length. The impatient tsar ordered his train into the lead and so the baggage section became the targeted "second train." Also the explosive expert Shiraev had foreseen rightly. The light dynamite charge would probably not have killed Alexander II anyway. The emperor commented poignantly on this fourth overt attempt at assassination:

"Am I such a wild beast that they should hound me to death?"

The Siege of the Winter Palace

Yes! was the reply of The People's Will in its underground newspaper:

"... until that time—war, implacable war, to the last drop of our blood!"

So it would be. Yet for the moment the terrorists were somewhat mollified. Their spectacular failure had captured the attention of the public. In their minds the phantasmal, deadly Executive Committee achieved prominence as a political terrorist force to be dealt with. And too, the committee found satisfaction in having come through the operation with only one casualty and with the fabric of the organization still hidden. But from that casualty a loose thread began to unwind . . .

Gregory Goldenberg had appeared in Odessa, collected the dynamite packed into a suitcase, and started back to Moscow. Apparently he checked the bag on his train, and a baggage

After passing through the three-part rail gauntlet in the fall of 1879, the tsar entered St. Petersburg triumphantly. (Sketch published in The Graphic, *December 20, 1879.)*

attendant noticed it was unusually heavy for its size. He told a policeman at the next stop and so on a railway platform in southern Russia, Goldenberg was asked to unlock and open the suitcase. A brief scuffle, a brief chase, and the terrorist courier was taken.

The earnest revolutionist was a man of courage, who steeled himself to resist bullying questioning, torture, death, as necessary. But when the police interrogator found him clamlike, he merely dismissed him and the new-caught prisoner found himself temporarily lodged in a cell with another revolutionist. Goldenberg's excitable nature caused him finally to pour out his anxieties—and much else—to this sympathetic companion who had turned police informer.

In future interviews with the police interrogator Goldenberg learned, without comprehending it came from his own loose talk, the extent of police knowledge of The People's Will and indeed the Executive Committee, too. Why, they knew everything! It was hopeless to continue the fight against such knowledgeable adversaries.

And then the gentle policeman intimated that many in surprisingly high places shared revolutionary aspirations, but not their bloody methods. Perhaps an armistice, an amnesty could be arranged . . . And so Goldenberg, imagining that he was bargaining for the lives of his friends, babbled on for months about the organization. He came to see himself in megalomaniac proportions as a bridge between extreme opponents, a savior, who could heal the festering national wound.

The People's Will would have been wiped out in short order if it had not been for the presence in Third Section police headquarters, St. Petersburg, of confidential clerk Nikolai Kletchnikov. He was the committee's early warning device, a credit

The Siege of the Winter Palace

to Mikhailov's security consciousness, which extended to not telling others—like Goldenberg—of the spy's existence.

Kletchnikov, a moralist, had been employed in the provincial government bureaucracy, found it stupid and grasping, and moved on to the capital seeking a better atmosphere at the office. But it was worse in St. Petersburg. Then the Janitor recruited the disillusioned civil servant.

The distant singing of Goldenberg alarmed Kletchnikov and he alerted Mikhailov: The police know everything! About all the plots, the names of the persons involved; in fact, the inside history of the organization going back to the middle seventies—who had killed whom, or tried to!

The Janitor was equal to the emergency, adeptly arranging the necessary internal changes to shield the organization's locale and activities. But a lot of damage had been done. Though the police still faced a difficult job in catching them, they now knew a great deal about the who and how of The People's Will.

Eventually Goldenberg was contacted in prison by a jailed former comrade who stripped away his grand delusion. From exultant self-confidence, the dupe plunged into total despair and, tearing a towel into strips, managed to hang himself from a metal fixture in his cell.

Meanwhile, the Executive Committee had thrust upon it another intriguing project to kill the tsar. Stepan Khalturin was an artisan with a background in labor organizing from the mid-seventies. But the stepped-up "white terror" of police oppression scattered the labor union and embittered Khalturin. He now resolved to murder Alexander II and believed he was in a prime position to do this because he both worked and *lived* in the royal Winter Palace!

But Khalturin needed dynamite to work his plot, and so

asked around until he was in contact with Mikhailov, the dynamite chairman of underground Russia. To the committee he explained that he and other workmen were lodged in a basement room. Two floors directly overhead was the royal dining room. A *mighty* dynamite charge set off in his room, Khalturin claimed, would penetrate to and kill occupants of the dining room.

The terrorists were certainly interested, but then the discussion turned to the occupants of the room in between the bomb and the tsar. It would be filled with ordinary people, being a barrack of the palace guardsmen, a Finnish unit. But in the end the self-righteousness of pure revolutionary purpose in The People's Will decided that an unknown number of the People could be sacrificed to get at the tsar.

A member of the committee began ferrying to the conspirator small amounts of dynamite secreted in clothing or beneath vegetables in a basket. For quite a while Khalturin stowed his slowly growing stock of explosives under his pillow. Then, in a potential disaster, the go-between was arrested and a floor plan of the palace discovered with an X marked on the dining room! But the police reaction was tepid. The area of the dining room was scrutinized, and there was a search of the worker's quarters too, but no one looked under Khalturin's pillow. There was absolutely no suspicion of Khalturin in the palace—indeed the head gendarme was trying to marry off his daughter to the bomb builder! The police pronounced the dining room secure and backed away.

Zhelyabov became the new dynamite courier and Executive Committee supervisor for the project. He seems not to have cared much for Khalturin, who in personality reminded him of Goldenberg. The palace plotter was visibly nervous and rundown from tension. Now he complained of violent nighttime headaches. Together they concluded this resulted from fumes emanating from the dynamite pillow. So the explosive was moved to his workman's chest, where it would surely be discovered in another search. It was urgent that the bomb be detonated soon.

But now Zhelyabov and Khalturin quarreled. The man on the inside insisted that more dynamite was required to do the job, while Zhelyabov, on the outside, obtained full committee support for an order to the bomb-maker to go ahead with the quantity on hand. Whether Zhelyabov's intuition was that Khalturin would go into nervous collapse and expose the plot, or whether his concerns were humanitarian—the bigger the blast the more innocent persons killed—is not known.

It was decided the explosion should occur during the emperor's dinner hour. He customarily went in at 5:30 P.M., but often delayed up to half an hour. The bomb's timing was to be set between 6:15 and 6:30 P.M. However, the assassination attempt was postponed from day to day because Khalturin could not obtain the needed privacy to set the timing apparatus. Each evening at about 6 P.M. the two conspirators passed in the great square before the Winter Palace and Khalturin made no sign of recognition to the impatient Zhelyabov. But on February 5, 1880, the bomb mechanic greeted his associate, and they stood together looking attentively at a particular set of glowing window panes in the palace across the square.

At 6:20 P.M., after a loud explosion, a cloud of dust and smoke jetted up from a section of the huge building and all of its lights went out. Confusion and dismay pervaded the disaster scene as horse-drawn ambulances and fire equipment galloped to the palace. The terrorists lingered as the dead and wounded were brought out, but they did not learn the fate of Alexander II

The Executive Committee tried to assassinate the tsar a fifth time by planting a bomb in the Winter Palace. This plan, too, failed. (Sketch published in L'Opinion Publique, *April 1, 1880.*)

The Siege of the Winter Palace

before an increasing police presence forced their withdrawal. Later at a hideout apartment Khalturin suffered a temporary nervous derangement. His agitation arose from fear of capture, not remorse.

What occurred inside the Winter Palace during the late afternoon and early evening of February 5?

Technically, the tsar's survival was guaranteed when the train bearing a minor central European ruler arrived late in St. Petersburg. This delayed his scheduled audience with Alexander II with the result that the royal dinner party was in a hallway when the blast cancelled their dining plans. Had they been seated at table they would have been terrified as the room vibrated violently, the china clattered to the floor, and sudden darkness fell. But they would have been unharmed. The bomb's lethal charge did not penetrate there. However, on the floor below there were eleven killed, fifty-six injured, both soldiers and civilians.

Khalturin bitterly blamed Zhelyabov for the botched opportunity. He was sent to Sweden for safety and later upon returning refused to work again for the committee so long as Andrei remained. It was another failure, a bloody one this time, but again the terrorists received a lot of publicity for their tiny band. And at least no one was arrested as a direct result of the bombing.

The Russian public and the world stood by amazed. The mysterious Executive Committee (two dozen persons and a printing press) appeared to be holding the emperor of Russia under siege in his own palace! To blow up the tsar's own dining room—how could this be possible without aid from within? The rumor factory went into overtime. And the fumbling police could not come up with even one new caught conspirator for a show trial and execution.

Alexander II had now had it with his police. He turned to the army and summoned General Loris-Melikov, a renowned war hero of Armenian descent, who as the current military governor at Kharkov had suppressed the revolutionists there and at the same time achieved a public popularity for open-minded fairness. The desperate tsar offered this soldier the post of dictator over the government of Russia.

General Loris-Melikov told the tsar that his acceptance was conditional. He could effectively nullify terrorist activity, he believed, but his technique depended up on a shift toward popular reform within the government. The mildly modern, democratic theories of the sixties must be brought forward. Regaining the trust and hope of the general public would result in the isolation of the small terrorist faction. Alexander II listened and warily agreed.

Wearily too—the emperor was haggard and exhausted. Though the tsar was personally fearless and fortified by abiding faith in his purpose and destiny, the frustrations and tensions of bracing for years against the unyielding demands of radical youth within his kingdom had been exceedingly wearing. Foreign negotiations and military missions also had not lived up to their promise for Russia during the past ten years. And then there was the terrible family mess he had willfully waded into and perpetuated. The affair of "Katia" had over the years isolated him from his wife and children and lost him the personal respect of a large majority of the ruling class within Russia.

Many monarchs were skirt-chasers, but most discreetly cavorted with a variety of mistresses for a season only. But Alexander II picked out Catherine (Katia) Dolgoruka as a teenage beauty in convent school and had been for fourteen years possessed by love for her. In 1874, he had acknowledged their perma-

The Siege of the Winter Palace

nent liaison (and the three children it had produced), declaring that Katia was "his wife before God" though dynastic considerations prevented a formal divorce from his royal wife.

The Empress Marie assumed a tight-lipped martyrlike attitude and now, after the palace bombing, had to put up with the presence of her husband's lover within the Winter Palace. The tsar's security aides had urged the move to cut out his daily trips to visit Katia. Terminally ill, the empress endured the knowledge that her husband had installed an elevator between his suite of rooms and Katia's one floor above.

Such unconventional and blatant actions outraged high society (for this was the Victorian era). Indeed, when the empress died that summer, Alexander II rushed into a nonroyal marriage with Katia and pondered how to install her as the new empress.

Alexander's son, the royal heir, now thirty-four and a straight-arrow husband and family man, was so disgusted with his father that he seriously considered abdicating his position and moving to Denmark. Earlier, one of the tsar's most able top police officials had departed through a similar distaste. Alexander II's popularity had waned among those who counted, and this was a probable factor in the aloofness of the middle and upper classes during the war between the emperor and the revolutionary terrorists. The institution of tsardom was as strong as ever, but its present occupant was in bad odor in St. Petersburg.

Loris-Melikov now proclaimed his "Dictatorship of the Heart" to the nation. He made some good moves. Hundreds of young people being held on flimsy pretexts or detained through unfeeling bureaucratic paper jams were released. The wretchedly conservative Minister of Education was replaced, curriculum and commentary somewhat loosened up. The secret police Third

General Loris-Melikov tried to quash the revolutionaries with a popular reform program, which he called his "Dictatorship of the Heart." (Sketch published in L'Opinion Publique, *April 5, 1880.)*

The Siege of the Winter Palace

Section itself was abolished. This was a cosmetic touch, for its body and functions, streamlined, were transferred elsewhere in the government.

The energetic subruler needed to be a cosmetician, for just below the government's surface was rock-hard conservatism and an emerging fear that he would go too far. Still he pleaded for some sort of conditional movement toward a constitutional government. Loris-Melikov wanted to convert the hesitant liberals into hopeful supporters of the regime. He began to talk about a consultative assembly convened from all responsible segments of the population. But toward the terrorists, he offered nothing but merciless eradication.

The People's Will realized that Loris-Melikov's intention toward them was as deadly as his predecessor's. Yet they hesitated, perhaps waiting to see how the educated classes would react to his proposals. When, early on, a radical named Ippolit Mlodetsky approached the Executive Committee with his intent to assassinate Loris-Melikov, they offered no objection but specified no support either.

In the style of the failed tsar-killer Soloviev, the young assassin accosted Loris-Melikov in the street, firing three times with a pistol. It was winter and the victim well-bundled in a massive overcoat. The small-bore bullets lodged in the sturdy collar. The doughty general pursued, captured, and subdued his assailant. He had the satisfaction in having him hanged within forty-eight hours, thereby showing the nation his skill and determination in meeting the enemies of the regime head-on. There followed a long lull in terrorist activity and Russia dared to believe and hope that Loris-Melikov's administration would prevail.

Loris-Melikov captured his would-be assassin, Mlodetsky, and saw him hanged within forty-eight hours. (Sketch published in L'Opinion Publique, April 15, 1880.)

The Siege of the Winter Palace

The terrorists had come through the palace bombing unscathed. So why were the bombs and pistols of the Executive Committee silent for the remainder of 1880?

Bad luck, sloppy follow-through, second thoughts about pushing terrorism before organizational expansion, a harrowing loss of personnel to a more efficient police offensive—these all together resulted in the unusual and deceptive quiet.

The government under Loris-Melikov reacted as if there were an army in St. Petersburg besieging the Winter Palace. Thousands of crack Cossack troops were imported into the capital where they were highly visible. The movements of Alexander II in and out of the Winter Palace were restricted as much as possible (a difficult and thankless job!). And intelligent use of Goldenberg's revelations coupled with efficient surveillance reduced the hard-core terrorists by at least one half during this year.

The first question to be decided by the Executive Committee was: Should they turn aside and strike personally at Loris-Melikov? No. The terrorists remained committed to killing the tsar. When they had eliminated the emperor, then Loris-Melikov would vanish in the anticipated general collapse of the government. Beside this, their resources did not allow the managing of two conspiratorial operations at the same time.

The committee turned back to a tactic of the recent past. It dispatched Sonia Perovskaya and a pseudo-husband to Odessa. They opened a grocery shop on the street leading to the dock where Alexander II would board his yacht when he came south that summer. A terrorist crew gathered, and energetic tunneling began in advance of a dynamite shipment. But then the death of the empress on May 22nd delayed or cancelled the Emperor's journey. The Odessa plotters wanted to blow up the regional military governor instead but were forbidden dynamite for that purpose. The buried mine way of death was reserved for the tsar, said the committee.

However, though Alexander II did not go south that summer, he certainly would spend time at Tsarskoe Selo, a favored royal palace about twenty miles outside St. Petersburg. The route from the Winter Palace crossed the Kammeny Bridge. Agents of the Executive Committee led by Andrei Zhelyabov installed in the water underneath the bridge four rubber containers holding a total of two hundred fifty pounds of dynamite. Wire and detonators were attached to the underside of a nearby floating dock used by washerwomen of the neighborhood.

The tsar's scheduled return from Tsarskoe Selo to the Winter Palace on August 17 was learned and at the hour Zhelyabov was at the raft awaiting an associate who would scrub a sack of potatoes as a diversionary tactic while Andrei arranged to set off the blast.

The other fellow arrived late—after the tsar had safely passed. He pleaded he had no timepiece. It *was* very Russian to be late for appointments, and the tardy one *was* a recent convert to the terrorist way of life/death, yet this mission sounds suicidal, so perhaps he had second thoughts about a personal sacrifice? Again, recalling Andrei's previous mechanical failure; maybe the wires were crossed again? The bridge mine was abandoned.

During that summer and fall a dissenting voice against total terrorism was raised in the policy discussions of The People's Will. The cautioner was Andrei Zhelyabov! The movement needed persuasive talkers more than they needed accomplished assassins, he believed. Not that Andrei was a relapsed terrorist: Kill the tsar? Yes, of course, but a bit later. They needed to think out more specifically how they could be ready to seize the levers

The Siege of the Winter Palace

of power after a royal assassination. They required more personnel, surely, and Zhelyabov, particularly, favored recruiting in the officer corps of the armed forces, a ready-made source of future revolutionary leadership. His eloquence had already lured some potential converts.

But he was outvoted in the Executive Committee, where policy was made by majority vote. The margin for total terrorism came through the votes of the several women members. In the beginning they had had to be coaxed into the terrorist faction, but now they were more bloodthirsty than the men! A participant remembered Sonia Perovskaya "in a soft childish voice proclaiming the necessity of terror."

Again that fall when news came in of crop failure in the south and a probable famine, Andrei called for a diversion. He wanted to go south and take this emergency opportunity to organize the peasants into a political unit. But again he was outvoted. The Executive Committee remained on its narrow course of tsaricide.

The terrorist compulsion was total after the "Trial of the Sixteen" in October of 1880. This group of revolutionists/terrorists had been arrested by Loris-Melikov's police in 1880 and included several members of the Executive Committee. All were dealt with harshly and two committee members were hanged. The executions of close comrades really stung in the organization. Revenge moved up from the background to become the obsessional force driving the shrinking band into a suicidal attack on Alexander II.

Then an aftermath event of the executions struck the most telling blow yet to the terrorist capabilities of the Executive Committee:

They lost the Janitor!

Mikhailov had been a close friend of one of the dead men and resolved to have a photograph of him reproduced as a memento. Word of this intent somehow reached the police, who set a watch on every photographer shop in St. Petersburg. A person in the shop Mikhailov visited attempted to warn him, and the Janitor, noting that he was followed upon leaving, took successful evasive action. Yet three days later, as scheduled, Mikhailov walked back into the shop to pick up the photo! And was taken by the police.

Why? The careful planner, the security-conscious veteran conspirator could not have been so gullible. Death as an option to complete a mission was a requirement of a thorough-going terrorist, and this willingness may have caused his downfall.

When Mikhailov was sentenced to death with several comrades at a trial long afterward, he is reported to have been serene, even looking forward to the final meeting on the gallows platform with his brothers in terror. But to his regret, his sentence was changed to life imprisonment. Cruelly, his jailers allowed him to suppose that he alone had been let off, while in fact the others also had been relieved of the death penalty. He died in prison of natural causes, willfully perhaps, within two years.

Stunned by the irreplaceable loss of their managing technician, the Executive Committee soon suffered another loss as well. Their spy in police headquarters, Kletchnikov, was taken. There would be no more advance warnings on police activities. Pushed back toward the brink of extinction, they looked to their new leader. He was Andrei Zhelyabov, whose job it now was to quickly direct and prepare them to carry through the most vital, the only mission they cared about anymore:

Kill the tsar!

V
EXECUTION!

Sometime in the fall of 1880, Andrei Zhelyabov and Sonia Perovskaya linked personally. They took a flat and lived the last months of their lives as man and wife though not formalizing the arrangement. The charisma of the tall, handsome Zhelyabov had at length melted the anti-male resolve of the formidable if petite Perovskaya. Vera Figner, a colleague on the Committee, said "Zhelyabov swept her off her feet." And her former boyfriend Lev Tikhomirov remarks in his memoirs:

> ... In the last year of [Sonia's] life she fell in love for the first time. It was Zhelyabov. She had always been a strong feminist and maintained that men were the inferior sex. She had real respect for very few of them. But Zhelyabov was up to her caliber. She was utterly in love with him, in a way I never thought could happen to her with any man ...

> ... Zhelyabov had a very high opinion of her intelligence and her character; as a colleague in the cause he felt she was incomparable. In their circumstances one cannot speak of "happiness." There was continual anxiety—not for each self but for the other —continual preoccupation, the unceasing rush of work which meant that they could scarcely ever be alone, the certainty that sooner or later there was bound to come a tragic ending. But there were times when the work was going well, when they were able to forget for a little and then it was a joy to see them, especially her. Her feeling was so overwhelming that in any but Perovskaya it would have crowded out all thoughts of her work ...

According to a subsequent police report, the couple lived quietly, receiving no mail and few visitors. They customarily emerged at dusk and returned long after midnight. Their home consisted of two small rooms and kitchen "furnished like the flat of a minor clerk in a government office"; a tacky tablecloth, muslin curtains, straw-stuffed cushions, cheap crockery in odd pieces, a samovar with a broken handle, all neatly kept. Several novels were found including a syrupy Victorian romance *Lost For Love* by Miss Braddon.

The union of Sonia with Andrei strengthened the leader's resolve for regicide. There would be no shilly-shallying, no relaxation in pushing toward the bloody climax. Sonia was surely as persuasive at home as at the Committee sessions.

During that fall Sonia had been in charge of a reconnaissance observing the movements of the tsar outside the Winter

Execution!

Palace. It was noted that his love of uniforms and military pomp often drew him to a particular parade ground on Sunday afternoons. The favored route followed the Nevsky Prospekt, the capital's Fifth Avenue, and then turned into the Malaya Sadovaya (Little Garden Street). The corner turn was tight, causing the coach to slow for it. And near there on Little Garden Street a basement shop was for lease!

By decree of the Executive Committee the basement at 4 Little Garden Street was leased, a bogus cheese shop installed, and the requisite tunnel started. The terrorist's insistence upon "blowing up" the Tsar was related to their expectation of the national political "explosion" they were certain would have to follow immediately upon the assassination.

But this time there would be a mop-up squad too. Supposing the explosion only disabled the coach or wounded the tsar? How should they kill the monarch before he escaped again into the Winter Palace?

Nikolai Kibalchich, their studious dynamite bomb manufacturer, had been reading the Royal Artillery Journal about techniques using nitroglycerine. He had thought it through and invented nitroglycerine hand bombs weighing about five pounds. Their explosive charge was not great; they would not be sufficient against objects. But hurled in a street confrontation they would be quite effective against bodies.

So the committee decided to have in place in the vicinity of the mined spot a bomb-equipped foursome to attack as necessary in the aftermath of the main explosion. Still remembering their numerous failures and the persistence of Alexander II's luck, they added one additional roving assassin to personally complete the regicide if necessary.

An out-of-town radical volunteered, but specified that he needed a shield of thirty comrades to cover the act. This was ludicrous—the total of committed terrorists in the capital was less than half this number. Then Andrei said *he* would be the last man in the tsar's murderous gauntlet. With a pistol in one hand a knife in the other, without cover, Zhelyabov proposed to dash in for the kill. By such a zealous outburst he hoped to deny the emperor another escape.

On the eve of 1881, The People's Will gathered for a party, a happy affair where for once no business was to be discussed. At first they were quiet amid thoughts of all the missing faces, imprisoned or dead. One party-goer who had witnessed a friend hanged in the south was fancifully grim as she fitted the noose and shroud to one and then another of her comrades. But gradually their somber comportment gave way to a contrasting mood of merriment, and though perhaps two-thirds of St. Petersburg was partying and drunk that New Year's Eve, the radicals' celebration became so infectiously raucous it attracted many in the neighborhood. It was the movement's last social hurrah. In the New Year all would be dead or scattered.

Preparations at Little Garden Street were well under way, but there were familiar problems. Though this tunnel was short, about twenty feet, it was in an urban setting. They had to be very careful about noise; and dirt disposal was impossible. It had to be stored in barrels and overflowed into piles on the basement floor, covered with straw or canvas.

Then the diggers encountered a major municipal conduit too thick to go under or over. They hoped it was only partially filled as they sliced into the top half. They were right, but choked in the realization they had opened a raw sewer line. The stench

Execution!

was overwhelming! Finally with makeshift gas masks allowing a very brief work period they succeeded in resealing the pipe in a way that allowed them to wriggle across the upper curvature.

Also the cheese shop was not functioning well as their necessary shield. The couple posing as the proprietors, Yuri Bogdanovich and Anna Yakimova (she was Andrei's "wife" at the Alexanderovsk attempt) did not exhibit the personalities expected of business-oriented small traders.

For one thing the "wife" dressed too bizarrely for her petty bourgeoise role and also insisted on smoking in public. The leftover cheeses in stock were not the popular sellers and buying more saleable cheese had nearly bankrupted the shrunken reserves at The People's Will. Business was poor because of another established cheese merchant in the neighborhood. This merchant thought that the sum of the parts of his new competitors did not add up to business sense. So, eventually, as the bomb site neared completion, the police made an official call.

The inspection was ineptly conducted as its leader, a general of the Corps of Engineers, listened passively to Bogdanovich's glib statements:

The barrels packed with tunnel earth he described as used to store cheese, and wetness on the floor caused by leakage from the barrels as a spill of milk from that morning. The straw covering other piles of dirt was used to pack the cheeses, Bogdanovich said. And when the inspector strode over to look at boards nailed onto a basement wall (to obscure the tunnel entrance), he was told it was to cover a bad crack where a damp draft oozed in. The general appeared poised to ask another question, or give an order, when—enter the conspiratorial cat!

She minced over and rubbed against the official boots purring with affection. The general stooped and began stroking his visitor. He was a cat lover! And in the style of Sonia at Moscow, the couple told a series of anecdotes about the almost-human traits of this unusual cat. The investigator listened appreciatively and soon departed the shop in good humor.

On Sunday afternoon, February 15, the coach of Alexander II had passed through Little Garden Street both going to and returning from the parade ground just as Sonia had said it would, but the terrorists were not ready. Explosive production was lagging, probably because of the added problem of fashioning the hand bombs. Now the committee firmly resolved that Sunday, March 1, would be the date of the tsar's execution.

It was in the selection of the bomb-throwers that the latter day Executive Committee showed deficiency. Zhelyabov did not choose high grade men. Of course Andrei did not wish to use up "our capital" of veteran personnel, already much depleted. And these men were put in expendable positions, for if the bomb-throwers went into action they were unlikely to come back.

Of the four selected, none appears to have had previous training or experience. Mostly they came from a goon squad in the worker's section that protected party interests in the mills. They were dazzled by Zhelyabov's oratorical brilliance, superficially inspired by the dark adventure of tsaricide. Their enthusiasm waxed and waned according to Zhelyabov's nearness.

Nikolai Rysakov, ex-engineering student, was just nineteen and, as coming events showed, in well over his head. Ignatei Grinevitski was a Pole of average background in the worker movement. Timothy Mikhailov, twenty, was a boiler maker, a beefy enforcer hindered by low intelligence. Ivan Emilianov, twenty, was a cabinetmaker who really *stood out* on the street

Execution!

being at least six inches taller than the average Russian, gangly and memorable. These were conscripts the Janitor would not have tolerated.

Zhelyabov's indifference to personnel had a prophetic precedent. For the Alexanderovsk attempt, he had also hired casual terrorist laborers. Now one of them, Ivan Okladski, in prison via Goldenberg's revelations, had replaced the former as a star police informer.

Overall, Loris-Melikov had reason for cautious optimism that his style of patchwork public administration was going to prevail. The terrorists had been silenced, and he knew from Okladski and his police that their ranks were thinning. Also it now appeared that his consultative assembly scheme for the government was going to be approved.

He had placated the conservative crown prince by indicating that the national congress-to-be was more show than substance; but he told the liberals that it was a new opening toward constitutional government. To the tsar he explained that the gesture would yield a spurt of needed personal popularity to help him put Katia over as the legal new empress. Loris-Melikov was a fixer all right and also understood the fix would disintegrate with another shot or bomb blast.

On February 20, the four new street assassins met in classroom setting with the professorial Kibalchich sketching the mechanism of the hand bombs on a blackboard as if he were teaching Applied Terrorist Physics I. On February 22, Zhelyabov took his squad to a remote spot to practice. The objects they hurled were dummies as the true bombs had yet to be manufactured. But one, half filled, was exploded for effect.

Meanwhile the police had been tipped, probably by Okladski, to watch the movements of Mikhail Trigoni, a radical based in Odessa who was a longtime friend of Zhelyabov's. Now he journeyed to St. Petersburg and the police followed him everywhere he went, noting the addresses he visited and installing a undercover man in the rooming house he stopped at.

The momentous result of this surveillance was that on February 27, Zhelyabov was captured in the rooming house! Not only captured but recognized by a police official who had served in the south:

"Why, you're Zhelyabov!"

"Your humble servant. But that is not going to help you," retorted Andrei.

Meeting in emergency session the available Executive Committee reviewed a bleak situation: Their leader had been taken. The cheese shop cover over the assassination site was being pondered by the police. The dynamite mine was not in place there nor had the supporting hand bombs been manufactured. And March 1 was the day after tomorrow!

Should they proceed?

Yes! It was unanimous, and a tight-lipped, implacable Sonia took over her lover's position as leader of the bomb-throwers.

Explosives wizard Nikolai Kibalchich now entered upon a seventeen-hour marathon of bomb production. First the dynamite charge for Little Garden Street was prepared and installed by Saturday evening. Then the delicate manufacture of the hand bombs proceeded by candlelight behind close-drawn curtains all Saturday night at a flat tenanted by a couple, Nikolai Sablin and Gesya Helfmann. Two bombs had been finished by Sunday morning and Sonia carried them, snugly wrapped in her apron, to a rendezvous cafe. The other two were delivered about noon. Each nitroglycerine grenade was disguised in white paper so that

Execution!

it resembled a large snowball. The bomb-throwers each received one and went to their positions on Little Garden Street.

Also on that Sunday morning the veteran terrorist Michael Frolenko dropped by Vera Figner's apartment at the breakfast hour. He was en route to Little Garden Street for he had been chosen to detonate the bomb. Frolenko was relaxed and imperturbable as was his style. He had brought bread, sausage, a bottle of wine, and his obvious enjoyment of the feast vexed Ms. Figner, who was in a state of tension, though she had been assigned a background support role in the operation.

In the Winter Palace, Alexander II arose at about 8:30 A.M. He was in a self-confident mood that day for two reasons: word had come from Loris-Melikov that the terrible Zhelyabov had been arrested. The terrorist claimed that he was only a third-level employee of the Executive Committee, but the police believed that they had landed a big fish. Also the cheese shop on Little Garden Street had been looked into and found to be just a cheese shop. Loris-Melikov advised the tsar to lie low in the Winter Palace a little while longer until the remainder of the gang could be picked up.

Also the monarch was upbeat today because he had at length ended his usual vacillation and signed the ukase establishing the consultative assembly. It would be announced to the nation the next day. The congress was to be chosen from responsible persons at varied levels of Russian society including the peasant organizations. Alexander II, in signing the decree, seemed to believe he was crossing a political watershed of importance:

"I have given my approval," he wrote, "but I do not hide from myself the fact that it is the first step toward a constitution."

The buoyant tsar was not put off from his afternoon plans by the entreaties of his wife to heed Loris-Melikov and stay at home. No! he would not be made a prisoner in his palace by a bunch of hoodlums. Katia extracted only the promise that he would not pass through Little Garden Street where that cheese shop was.

In the early afternoon Michael Frolenko stood impassively on a table in the cheese shop basement holding the detonator wires and peering through the high, narrow cellar window at the explosion site. Since he was near the tunnel entrance and thereby a short twenty feet from eighty pounds of dynamite, his survival chances were as dubious as those of neighbors and pedestrians. Mass murder was again at risk.

Frolenko had stood thus for some time and now called out to Anna Yakimova who was out front at the store counter and also his lookout to announce the approach of the royal coach. He noted that the tsar was a long time coming!

Ms. Yakimova stepped outside and looked around the corner. Returning she reported that the emperor was passing by another route, along the Catherine Canal. Thereupon Frolenko packed his gear and went home. Kibalchich, lingering nearby to witness the effect of his handiwork, also turned back when he saw the direction the tsar was going. There had been so many failures! It was easy to give in to another.

Only Sonia Perovskaya remained steadfast to carry through the terrorist's obsession to kill the tsar!

She rallied her troops and sketched out alternative positions on the back of an envelope. Sonia specifically instructed each of her four bomb hurlers on what to do and where to be according to the tsar's return route. She told them she would signal appropriately by blowing her nose in a handkerchief. She pointed out her viewpoint on the other side of the canal. Then it was all up to them!

Execution!

When the emperor's coach and escorts emerged from the parade ground Sonia realized immediately that the return to the Winter Palace would again be by way of the Catherine Canal. A slim, determined figure in the flat winter daylight, she hurried to signal her bomb-throwers. Had Alexander II come straight on, he would have passed before his assailants could reach him, but he halted for a quarter-hour visit with a favorite cousin. When he came on the bomb gauntlet had formed—Mikhailov, Rysakov, Grinevitski, and Emilianov, spaced out along the canal quay, each lounging as casually as he could and holding a white package underarm. Except that now Mikhailov had belated second thoughts; he walked away and turned in his bomb to Gesya Helfmann at the committee's munitions apartment.

Perhaps the coachman had an intuition, for as he entered the canal area he whipped up the horses into a light gallop. The mounted Cossack guard (two of whom rode on either side outside the coach doors) fell back a bit. Rysakov threw his bomb a little late. It exploded beneath and just behind the royal coach. A sharp report, a geyser of smoke and snow spray and immediately screams of pain from a downed Cossack and a writhing passerby, a delivery boy from a butcher shop. Both soon died.

The armored coach, though damaged, remained operational and the coachman began to urge the frightened horses into a dash for the palace. But Alexander II ordered a halt and got out shaken and lightly cut by shattered glass. Security personnel from a trailing sleigh came up and begged him to continue to the palace. He refused and walked back to the explosion scene to see the wounded and confront the captured assassin. Exactly what was said and happened next varies by eyewitness account. Here is the sense of it.

The tsar approached his attacker, leaving himself vulnerable to the successful attempt by Grinevitski. (Sketch published in The Graphic, March 26, 1881.)

Grinevitski walked up to the tsar and dropped his bomb, effectively killing Tsar Alexander II and himself. (Sketch published in The Graphic, *March 26, 1881.)*

A crowd, attracted by the explosion, was thickening at the site and someone asked if the tsar were injured?

"I am safe, thank God," the monarch replied, "but see the others here!"

"Still thanking God?"

This from Rysakov, who received a blow to the face by one of his captors for his insolence. The tsar now approached Rysakov and asked if he had thrown the bomb?

"Yes."

"What is your name?"

"Glazov, artisan."

"A fine fellow!"

Alexander II turned curtly and walked to inspect the shallow bomb crater. The crowd was tightly encircling him now. Satisfied, he was being urged to board the sleigh and leave the scene. He began walking toward it. Just then a man with a white package, who had been leaning against the canal parapet, turned and stepped to confront the tsar. Then Grinevitski dropped his bomb at their feet.

In an instant, regent and regicide lay horribly, mortally mangled, and flattened round the principals were about twenty other casualties from the crowd.

A nearby witness was Emilianov, the fourth bomb thrower.

Now he was taken with a very human compulsion and, with his bomb carefully cradled under one arm, rushed to the tsar's side and by his account was actually one of those who helped carry the emperor to the sleigh!

Grand Duke Constantine, who had been at the parade ground too, now arrived and bent over his maimed brother.

"Cold, cold," murmured the tsar; then: "To the palace . . . to die there."

Both Alexander II and his assassin died by evening, the latter without revealing his name. But the police held Rysakov and he was no match for them. The same interrogator (since promoted) who had skillfully debriefed Goldenberg was set on Rysakov and in a short period of days the police had, without torture, wrung from him all the conspiratorial knowledge that he possessed.

Sonia saw it all across the narrow canal. She was able to keep a 2:30 P.M. appointment at a cafe and told her colleagues quietly in short, simple sentences that she believed this seventh assassination attempt by the Executive Committee had been successful.

Vera Figner records a more ecstatic reaction in her memoirs:

> . . . *When I entered my own dwelling and saw my friends who as yet suspected nothing, I was so agitated that I could hardly utter the words announcing the death of the tsar. I wept, and many of us wept; that heavy nightmare, which for ten years had strangled young Russia before our very eyes, had been brought to an end; the horrors of prison and exile, the violence, executions, and atrocities inflicted*

Execution!

on hundreds and thousands of our adherents, the blood of our martyrs, all were atoned for by this blood of the tsar, shed by our hands. A heavy burden was lifted from our shoulders; reaction must come to an end and give place to a new Russia

The terrorist's euphoria did not last forty-eight hours. In the prison Rysakov was talking, at first resisting, but then carelessly passing information he considered ordinary into attentive, patient police ears. They soon had reason to revisit the cheese shop. The investigators found it abandoned with the dynamite mine in place. On the front counter Anna Yakimova had left a note and a bit of money: Take care of our cat, please!

The police obtained the address of the munitions apartment and raided it on Monday night. Gesya Helfmann responded by voice to their official door pounding but did not open up. Instead two bullets slammed out through the door panel. Taking cover, the police returned fire in a sporadic gun battle. Soon however Helfmann's screams announced that she had found her comrade Nikolai Sablin dead. He had shot himself with his last revolver round. In the apartment the two remaining live nitroglycerine bombs were recovered.

A watch was then set, in familiar police fashion, on this apartment building. Into the trap walked Timothy Mikhailov, the lapsed bomb-thrower. The terrorist pulled a revolver and wounded two policemen before, with great restraint, he was subdued alive. In prison he exercised stolid stupidity, and interrogators learned nothing of value from him. Emilianov, the kindly bomb-thrower, had left the city (as had the cheese shop couple) and was free for about a year.

In the aftermath of the assassination a few workers' group

Following up on Rysakov's information, the police dig out the bomb tunnel on Little Garden Street. (Sketch published in L'Illustration, April 2, 1881.)

Execution!

leaders contacted the committee asking if there were plans for insurrection? There were none. It had been a revenge killing. The surviving terrorists were exhausted and amazed at having succeeded at committing regicide. The committee (probably Lev Tikhomirov) did address a letter to the new Tsar Alexander III.

In tone its assumption was that of communication between equals. It said in effect: We're sorry we had to kill your father to gain the attention of the government to our demands. You can understand now how serious we are about them. Please do make some major moves toward turning the government over to the People. In this way *you* may be able to survive our surveillance of your policies.

There was no reply from Alexander III, and of course his father's approval of the consultative assembly was not revealed. This was no time to show weakness! The government was intent on rounding up the remaining killers and associates. Then there must be a full show trial and executions. Only after this was accomplished could the new tsar begin to gain assurance that he would not be murdered too.

Directing the bomb throwers to their target on the Catherine Canal quay was the last important, the final rational service that Sonia Perovskaya performed for the Executive Committee. From the obsession of tsaricide she passed to a total but futile focus on freeing her lover. None of her rescue schemes were practical, but were generated by sheer desire. She clung to the wishful belief that because Zhelyabov was in prison at the hour of the attack he would not be charged with complicity in it. Now Andrei himself removed that far-fetched possibility.

In prison, with very limited sources of information, Zhelyabov made an important decision. He knew the tsar was dead, but also that revolutionary mobs were not assaulting his jail to set the assassins free. He had been confronted by Rysakov and believed he was the only conspirator/assassin captured. Zhelyabov thought now they might put this inexperienced youth on trial alone and he would probably not make a great impression upon the watching world.

For Zhelyabov prison rot stretched into infinity. But he knew to be meaningful to their movement, the trial would need *a talker* who would expound the creed and causes of radical revolution with fluency. He determined on self-sacrifice and penned a very self-incriminating confession which included a threat against the new Alexander. He made sure he would be there beside Rysakov.

A companion has recalled how, while walking on the Nevsky Prospekt, Sonia purchased the newspaper that informed her that Zhelyabov had voluntarily, triumphantly confessed. She turned aside, tears welling, the paper trailing from her fingers. At twenty-six, after a decade of service in the movement, the pragmatic terrorist had been undone by love. She continued to drift, turning aside opportunities to escape from Russia.

The miserable Rysakov was now fully cooperative and provided a description of the bomb squad leader he knew only as "the blonde" which police investigation determined to be Perovskaya. They found a market woman who knew the fugitive as a customer and who agreed to cruise the city with a detective. Thereby Sonia was captured at midday riding in a horse cab on the capital's main avenue. Rysakov positively identified her.

Now Kibalchich, the explosives wizard, was betrayed by his landlady and immediately afterward the police captured Frolenko too. He walked unknowing into the police trap at Kibalchich's flat. Rysakov identified the bomb-maker but he had not met Frolenko. So this veteran plotter was let out of the assassina-

Collage of the regicide defendants, clockwise from top left: Mikhailov, Hessy Helfmann, Sonia Perovskaya, Rysakov, evidence and exhibits, the president of the High Court, Kibalchich, and, in the center, Andrei Zhelyabov, "the talker." (Sketch published in *L'Illustration*, April 23, 1881.)

tion trial and the noose. An imperturbable player with whatever cards life dealt him, Frolenko survived over twenty years in the worst prisons of the tsars. He emerged, witnessed the Russian Revolution, lived on and on into the era of World War II (as did Anna Yakimova). It is said that Stalin forced Frolenko, at the age of eighty-eight, to join the Communist Party.

The assassin's trial began on March 26 and lasted three days before a tribunal that was neither military nor secret. The regime was not concerned about the verdict. It would be guilty with the death penalty. So this court's sessions were public and reported and the six defendants—Zhelyabov, Perovskaya, Kibalchich, Mikhailov, Helfmann, and Rsyakov—had the benefit of defense counsel as desired and the opportunity to voice their opinions.

Zhelyabov ably used his speaking time for the teaching and justification of revolution. Perovskaya indignantly repudiated the charge that their action had been "immoral," taking the position that those who kill to benefit humanity are honoring a higher principle. Kibalchich was primarily concerned that his advanced theories for manned flight via rocketry not be ignored. Mikhailov said he had joined the terrorists "to kill spies and bad bosses." Rysakov claimed that he was a misled pacifist. And Helfmann announced that she was pregnant.

At trial's end five terrorists received death sentences. Helfmann was given a prison sentence due to the child in her body. It would be born in prison and soon die along with its mother of natural causes. Because of the aristocratic lineage of Perovskaya, the tsar's permission was needed and granted for her execution. Sonia's mother visited and comforted her, and she was gratified by being able to sit with Zhelyabov at the trial sessions.

April 3 was a fair day and a crowd of one hundred thousand, generally hostile to the condemned, thronged the execution

The execution scene as depicted in L'Illustration, *April 30, 1881.*

ground. At 8:50 A.M. the carts bearing the prisoners reached the scaffold platform upon which five black wooden coffins were stacked behind the hanging nooses. Priests climbed up and all the tsaricides kissed the crucifix and four embraced one another in farewell, ignoring the wretched Rysakov. Each was then robed in a blanket-like garment.

The execution proceeded as a botched affair. Hanging in Russia was by primitive strangulation. On this occasion the hangman was drunk and there were slipped knots necessitating rehangings. All met death with stoic courage except Rysakov. He was the last, and struggled vainly as he was grasped into the noose. Probably he had hoped for a reprieve on the gallows for his cooperation.

Within the hour all the bodies were taken down and placed in their coffins. The crowd was allowed to surge forward in its frenzy for souvenirs. Vera Figner, one of the few Executive Committee stalwarts not arrested at this time, indignantly recalled:

> ... I happened to take a horse-car in which there were people returning from the Semenovsky Square where the execution had taken place. Many faces were excited, but there was no sign of regret or sorrow. Just across from me there sat a good-looking burgher in a blue overcoat. He was black-haired and swarthy, with a bristling beard and glowing eyes. His handsome face was distorted with passion; a real *oprichnik* he was, ready to hew off heads.

After all the struggle and the agony of decades, had anything in Russia changed? In the war between the tsar and the terrorists, had either won?

Conclusion
Afterward

Alexander III nullified the decree of his father establishing a consultative assembly, and soon Loris-Melikov was maneuvered into resigning his job along with the few liberal-leaning ministers in the government. The new tsar reestablished the ancient union of purpose between the government and the nobility. He proclaimed he would govern "with faith in the might and justice of autocratic rule which for the good of the people we are called to strengthen and defend from encroachment."

What did "the People" think? The middle and upper classes were lulled because Alexander III was more adept at promoting industry and commerce than his father had been. Anyway, it was extremely risky to speak out against the regime. The ears of the police were always listening. As for the peasantry, they would be losers, with the landowners again partners with the regime. A kind of distraction was offered by the pogroms against Russian Jews that began at this time.

The peasants did not waver in their traditional veneration of tsardom. Many believed that Alexander II had been killed *by the nobles* because he had attempted to help the people too much. In another version God had protected the tsar through the other assassination attempts because he was good but had abandoned him when he turned bad. In any case they looked trustfully toward the new tsar.

Alexander III, described as "having the mind of a policeman," labored mightily to reinforce the security of the state. An efficient and powerful police organization finished off the Executive Committee in a few years. At one point *the leader* of the harried terrorists was a police spy! Thereafter "the peace of the graveyard" shrouded politics in Russia for a generation. And this efficiently autocratic tsar died in bed.

Oscar Wilde observed: "A thing is not necessarily true because a man dies for it." In this time of "peace," did the survivors of The People's Will regret their program of terrorism? Vera Figner had ample time—about twenty years in tsarist prisons—to contemplate the subject. Afterward she reasoned:

> *... Violence, whether committed against a thought, an action, or a human life, never contributed to the refinement of morals. It arouses ferocity, develops brutal instincts, awakens evil impulses, and prompts acts of disloyalty. Humanity and magnanimity are incompatible with it. And from this point of view, the government and the revolutionary party, when they entered into what may be termed a hand-to-hand*

battle, vied with one another in corrupting everything and every one around them. On the one hand the party declared that all methods were fair in the war with its antagonist, that here the end justified the means. At the same time it created a cult of dynamite and the revolver, and crowned the terrorist with a halo; murder and the scaffold acquired a magnetic charm for the youth of the land . . . . Since the effects of ideas are hardly perceptible to a revolutionist during the brief span of his lifetime, he desires to see some concrete, palpable manifestation of his own will, his own strength, and at that time only a terroristic act with all its violence could be such a manifestation.

After a discourse on the mindless brutality of the government as seen from her side, Figner reaffirms the old radical theme that the end justified their means.

The People's Will sacrificed or wasted itself upon the means. Did it attain its ends at all?

Certainly not in 1881, or for decades afterward. As Plekhanov had predicted at the populist congress that sentenced the tsar to death, all that had happened in that act was placing a "III" after Alexander. Probably though, Zhelyabov and company did give the history of an unknown future "a push" down the years.

The faint-hearted liberalism of Alexander II was the last to be seen in Old Russia. The best opportunity, wan as it was, for a normal thaw in Russian absolutism died with him. The lid was clamped down with vengeance thereafter. The nation may then be likened to a teakettle that has been sealed without turning down the heat of popular discontent. No steam can escape until the time of the *explosion*. Then, in 1917, every part of the former life in Russia was blown away.

The Soviet regime, approving the heroes/martyrs of The People's Will, has memorialized them in Leningrad's (formerly St. Petersburg) place names. Right by the Winter Palace is Khalturin Street recalling the palace bomber. Herzen and Plekhanov Streets remember gurus of the revolutionary movement. A few blocks from the Winter Palace is broad, tree-lined Zhelyabov Street, a shopping avenue of downtown. And paralleling it just a block away is the shorter Perovskaya Street. Thus Andrei and Sonia remained linked in municipal geography as they were in life.

A POPULAR BIBLIOGRAPHY

In The Name Of The People—Adam B. Ulam.
  A thorough, readable review of prerevolutionary Russia compiled from original sources by a scholar of mildly conservative outlook.
Roots Of Revolution—Franco Venturi.
  A scholarly history of the varied radical groups active in 19th-century Russia and biased toward their objectives.
The Fortress—Robert Payne.
  A detailed popular treatment of the era.
The Alexander Conspiracy—David Footman.
  A compassionate biography of Andrei Zhelyabov
The Emperor Alexander II—C. M. Almedingen.
  A standard informational biography

INDEX

Alexander II, Tsar, 11-12
  assassinated, 103-10
  first assassination attempt,
    22-23
  second assassination attempt,
    25
  third assassination attempt,
    60-61
  fourth assassination attempt,
    70-78
  fifth assassination attempt,
    81-85
  and Katia, 86-87
  offensive against revolutionaries, 46-47
  and political radicalism of young, 13-25
  sentenced to death by Executive Committee, 66, 68
Alexander III, Tsar, 113, 119-20
Arson in Russian cities, 16

Bakunin, Michael, 32-33, 34
The Black Repartition, 68
Bogdanovich, Yuri, 99
Bogishich, Professor, 31
Bogishich incident, 31

Censorship, loosened, 11
Chaikovsky Circle, 29, 35
Chernyshevsky, N. G., 16-20
  children of, 7-25

Index

Civic execution, 19-20
Commune, 29-30
Constantine, Grand Duke, 110

Death or Freedom faction, 47-49, 56, 65-66
Dictatorship of the Heart, 87-89
Dostoevski, 35
Drenteln, General, 58, 60

Education, 10-12
Emancipation, 1861, 7, 9-10
Emilianov, Ivan, 100, 105, 109-10, 111
Execution, civic, 19-20
Executive Committee, 60-62, 66, 68, 69, 71-75, 79, 80-85, 91, 93, 97, 100, 102, 120
Exile to Siberia, 19

Fathers and Sons (Turgenev), 12
Figner, Vera, 70, 95, 103, 110-11, 118, 120-21
Fortress/prison of Sts. Peter and Paul, 48
Frolenko, Michael, 54, 62-64, 70, 103, 104, 114-16

Gogol, 11
Goldenberg, Gregory, 59, 75-76, 79-81
Grinevitski, Ignatei, 100, 105-9

Hartmann, Lev, 72-74, 77
Helfmann, Gesya, 102, 105, 111, 115, 116
Herzen, Alexander, 33
Heyking, Baron, 52-53

Ishutin, Nikolai, 21-24
Ivanov, Ivan, 34

Karakozov, Dmitri, 21-23
Khalturin, Stepan, 81-85
Kibalchich, Nikolai, 69, 97, 101, 102, 104, 114-16
Kletchnikov, Nikolai, 80-81, 94
Kobilyanski, Louis, 59
Kolgoruka, Catherine (Katia), 86-87, 101, 104
Kommissarov, Ossip, 22-25
Kornilov sisters, 28
Kovalsky, 49
Kravchinsky, Serge, 52, 55-56
Kropotkin, Prince Dmitri, 53
Kropotkin, Prince Peter, 53-54

Land, distribution, and Emancipation, 9-10
Land and Liberty organization, 47-52, 56-57, 59, 68
  Death or Freedom faction, 47-49, 56, 65-66
Lavrov, P. L., 35-36
Lebedeva, Tatiana, 70
Lizogub, Dmitri, 64

Index

Loris-Melikov, General, 86-91, 101, 103, 119
Lost for Love (Braddon), 96

Marie, Empress, 87
Mezentsev, General, 52
Michaelis, 19
Mikhailov, Alexander, 47-52, 57-68, 74, 81, 94
Mikhailov, Timothy, 100, 105, 111, 115, 116
Mirski, Leon, 58-59
Mlodetsky, Ippolit, 89-90
Morozov, Nikolai, 47-49, 56, 75
Myshkin, 54-55

Nechaev, Sergei, 32-34, 58, 62
Nihilists, 12
Nobel, Alfred, 69

Okladski, Ivan, 101
The Organization, 21-25
Osinski, Valerian, 42, 52-54, 62, 64

The People's Will, 4-6, 68, 78-79, 80-82, 89, 98, 120, 121
Perovskaya, Sophia (Sonia), 4, 7, 10-11, 23, 27-30, 36-37, 42-43, 47, 54-56, 67-68, 72-76, 91, 93, 95-96, 104-5, 110, 113-16
Perovski, General, 23, 27

Pisarov, Dmitry, 12
Plekhanov, Georgy, 66-67, 121
Police, Third Section, 47, 62, 80, 89
The Possessed (Dostoevski), 35

Radicalism, political, of young, 12-25
Repression following assassination attempt, 26
"The Revolutionary Catechism" (Nechaev), 33-34
Royal Artillery Journal, 97
Rysakov, Nikolai, 100, 105, 108, 110, 111-16, 118

Sablin, Nikolai, 102, 111
St. Petersburg University, 14
Serfdom, 8-10
Shiraev, Stepan, 77, 78
Soloviev, Alexander, 59-63
Students, jailed for radicalism, 14-16
Sudeykin, Colonel, 53

Tikhomirov, Lev, 47-49, 56-57, 62, 95, 113
Tolstoi, Count, Minister of Education, 31
Trepov, Feodor, 43-45
Trepov affair, 43-45
Trial of the 193, 42-43, 45, 46
Trial of the Sixteen, 93

Index

Trigoni, Mikhail, 101
Tsaricide, 3-6
Tunnel, 72-77
Turgenev, Ivan, 12, 16

Universities, and radicalism of the young, 14-16

What Is to Be Done? (Chernyshevsky), 17-18
Wilde, Oscar, 120
Winter Palace bombing, 81-85
Women, education, 11

Yahnenko, Olga, 42
Yakimova, Anna, 70, 99, 104, 111, 116
Young, political radicalism, 12-25
Youth social study/action groups, 35-36

Zazulich, Vera, 32, 33, 44-45, 46
Zhelyabov, Andrei, 4, 7-10, 23, 29, 30-32, 40-43, 62-68, 70-72, 76, 82-85, 92-98, 100-102, 113-16